MERN Quick Start Guide

Build web applications with MongoDB, Express.js, React, and Node

Eddy Wilson Iriarte Koroliova

BIRMINGHAM - MUMBAI

MERN Quick Start Guide

Commissioning Editor: Ashwin Nair
Acquisition Editor: Nigel Fernandes
Content Development Editor: Roshan Kumar
Technical Editor: Shweta Jadhav
Copy Editor: Safis Editing
Project Coordinator: Hardik Bhinde
Proofreader: Safis Editing
Indexer: Rekha Nair
Graphics: Jason Monteiro
Production Coordinator: Shantanu Zagade

First published: May 2018

Production reference: 1310518

Published by Packt Publishing Ltd.
Livery Place
35 Livery Street
Birmingham
B3 2PB, UK.

ISBN 978-1-78728-108-0

www.packtpub.com

`mapt.io`

Mapt is an online digital library that gives you full access to over 5,000 books and videos, as well as industry leading tools to help you plan your personal development and advance your career. For more information, please visit our website.

Why subscribe?

- Spend less time learning and more time coding with practical eBooks and Videos from over 4,000 industry professionals

- Improve your learning with Skill Plans built especially for you

- Get a free eBook or video every month

- Mapt is fully searchable

- Copy and paste, print, and bookmark content

PacktPub.com

Did you know that Packt offers eBook versions of every book published, with PDF and ePub files available? You can upgrade to the eBook version at `www.PacktPub.com` and as a print book customer, you are entitled to a discount on the eBook copy. Get in touch with us at `service@packtpub.com` for more details.

At `www.PacktPub.com`, you can also read a collection of free technical articles, sign up for a range of free newsletters, and receive exclusive discounts and offers on Packt books and eBooks.

Contributors

About the author

Eddy Wilson Iriarte Koroliova has worked and led the development of a SaaS web application for the financial sector in 2012 with the LAMP stack for 4 years. Since 2014, he has been working as a senior full-stack developer and JavaScript specialist with the MERN stack, for the development of enterprise web applications for different sectors.

Eddy travels frequently and mostly works remotely. He speaks Spanish, English, and Russian, and he is currently learning Chinese, which has allowed him to work in different team environments and communicate better with clients and co-workers.

Special thanks to my partner in life, Huang Jingxuan, for always being there and for supporting me not only while writing this book but also during the different stages of my life and development of my career.
A big thank you to my family for their moral and financial support while starting my career as a developer.

About the reviewer

Chance is passionate about the intersection of technology, collaboration, and education. He is the founder of Chingu, a global collaboration platform for tech-learners, which has brought together thousands of developers, designers, and data scientists from 140 countries to learn and build together.

> *I'd like to thank Eddy Wilson for writing this book, Simon Van den Broeck for his edit contributions, and the Chingu community!*

Packt is searching for authors like you

If you're interested in becoming an author for Packt, please visit authors.packtpub.com and apply today. We have worked with thousands of developers and tech professionals, just like you, to help them share their insight with the global tech community. You can make a general application, apply for a specific hot topic that we are recruiting an author for, or submit your own idea.

Table of Contents

Preface

The MERN stack can be seen as a collection of tools that share a common denominator that is the language, JavaScript. The book explores, in the form of recipes, how to build web client and server applications using the MERN stack following the MVC architectural pattern.

The model and controller of the MVC architectural pattern are covered by the chapters about building RESTful APIs with ExpressJS and Mongoose. The chapters cover core concepts about the HTTP protocol, type of methods, status codes, URLs, REST, and CRUD operations. Afterward, it moves to topics specific to ExpressJS, such as request handlers, middleware, and security, as well as specific topics about Mongoose, such as schemas, models, and custom validation.

The view of the MVC architectural patterns is covered by the chapter about ReactJS. ReactJS is a UI library that is component-based with a declarative API. The book's aim to provide the essential knowledge for building ReactJS web applications and components. Complementary to ReactJS, the book contains an entire chapter about Redux that explains from the very core concepts and principles to advanced features such as store enhancers, time travelling, and asynchronous data flow.

Additionally, this book covers real-time communication with ExpressJS and SocketIO to deliver and exchange data in real time.

By the end of the book, you will know the core concepts and essentials for building full-stack web applications with the MVC architectural pattern.

What this book covers

Chapter 1, *Introduction to MERN Stack*, provides an introduction to the MERN stack and the MVC architectural pattern. It covers installation of NodeJS and MongoDB as well as installing NPM packages and an example of usage. These constitute the base for all the book's recipes.

Chapter 2, *Building a Web Server with ExpressJS*, covers core concepts about the HTTP protocol, the "http" NodeJS module, and how it is all connected with ExpressJS. It explores all features of ExpressJS for building Web Server applications from route handlers and middleware to secure a Web Server application and debugging.

Chapter 3, *Building a RESTful API*, explains core concepts about what is REST, URLs, and CRUD operations. These concepts are the base for the whole chapter. It also explores how to make CRUD operations in ExpressJS and with Mongoose as well as where and how ExpressJS and Mongoose fit in the MVC architectural pattern. It covers the creation of Mongoose schemas and models as well as different types of Mongoose middleware and validation of data.

Chapter 4, *Real-time Communication with Socket.IO and ExpressJS*, gives a brief introduction to NodeJS events and how bi-directional communication with WebSockets works. It also goes through using SocketIO and ExpressJS to build Web Applications that deliver data in real time.

Chapter 5, *Managing State with Redux*, covers what Redux is and the three core principles. It also covers the very basic idea of Redux from how Array.prototype.reduce works, to how reducers are defined and how to write middleware functions as well as advanced concepts such as writing store enhancers, time traveling, and asynchronous data flow.

Chapter 6, *Building Web Applications with React*, explains what React is, what JSX syntax is, and where in the MVC architectural pattern it fits. It explores all core concepts of React in the form of easy-to-follow and build recipes. The recipes cover topics about composition, life cycle methods, controlled and uncontrolled components, error boundary components, and others such as type checking with PropTypes and Portals.

To get the most out of this book

This book is for developers who are interested in getting started with the MERN stack for developing web applications. In order to be able to understand the chapters, you should have already a general knowledge and understanding of the JavaScript language.

What you need for this book

In order to be able to work on the recipes, you need the following:

- An IDE or code editor of your preference. Visual Studio Code (vscode) was used when writing the recipes' codes, so I suggest you to give it a try
- An Operating System (O.S) that is able to run NodeJS and MongoDB, preferably one of the following:
  - macOS X Yosemite/El Capitan/Sierra
  - Linux
  - Windows 7/8/10 (.NET framework 4.5 is required if installing VSCode in Windows 7)
- Preferably, at least 1 GB RAM and 1.6 GHz processor or faster

Download the example code files

You can download the example code files for this book from your account at `www.packtpub.com`. If you purchased this book elsewhere, you can visit `www.packtpub.com/support` and register to have the files emailed directly to you.

You can download the code files by following these steps:

1. Log in or register at `www.packtpub.com`.
2. Select the **SUPPORT** tab.
3. Click on **Code Downloads & Errata**.
4. Enter the name of the book in the **Search** box and follow the onscreen instructions.

Once the file is downloaded, please make sure that you unzip or extract the folder using the latest version of:

- WinRAR/7-Zip for Windows
- Zipeg/iZip/UnRarX for Mac
- 7-Zip/PeaZip for Linux

The code bundle for the book is also hosted on GitHub at `https://github.com/PacktPublishing/MERN-Quick-Start-Guide`. In case there's an update to the code, it will be updated on the existing GitHub repository.

We also have other code bundles from our rich catalog of books and videos available at `https://github.com/PacktPublishing/`. Check them out!

Download the color images

We also provide a PDF file that has color images of the screenshots/diagrams used in this book. You can download it here: `https://www.packtpub.com/sites/default/files/downloads/MERNQuickStartGuide_ColorImages.pdf`.

Code in Action

Visit the following link to check out videos of the code being run: `https://goo.gl/ymdYBT`

Conventions used

There are a number of text conventions used throughout this book.

`CodeInText`: Indicates code words in text, database table names, folder names, filenames, file extensions, pathnames, dummy URLs, user input, and Twitter handles. Here is an example: "Mount the downloaded `WebStorm-10*.dmg` disk image file as another disk in your system."

A block of code is set as follows:

```
{
    "dependencies": {
      "express": "4.16.3",
      "node-fetch": "2.1.1",
      "uuid": "3.2.1"
    }
}
```

Any command-line input or output is written as follows:

```
npm install
```

Bold: Indicates a new term, an important word, or words that you see onscreen. For example, words in menus or dialog boxes appear in the text like this. Here is an example: "Select **System info** from the **Administration** panel."

 Warnings or important notes appear like this.

 Tips and tricks appear like this.

Sections

In this book, you will find several headings that appear frequently (*Getting ready*, *How to do it...*, *Let's test it...*, *How it works...*, *There's more...*, and *See also*).

To give clear instructions on how to complete a recipe, use these sections as follows:

Getting ready

This section tells you what to expect in the recipe and describes how to set up any software or any preliminary settings required for the recipe.

How to do it...

This section contains the steps required to follow the recipe.

Let's test it...

This section consists of detailed steps on how to test the code given in *How to do it...* section.

How it works...

This section usually consists of a detailed explanation of what happened in the previous section.

There's more...

This section consists of additional information about the recipe in order to make you more knowledgeable about the recipe.

See also

This section provides helpful links to other useful information for the recipe.

Get in touch

Feedback from our readers is always welcome.

General feedback: Email `feedback@packtpub.com` and mention the book title in the subject of your message. If you have questions about any aspect of this book, please email us at `questions@packtpub.com`.

Errata: Although we have taken every care to ensure the accuracy of our content, mistakes do happen. If you have found a mistake in this book, we would be grateful if you would report this to us. Please visit `www.packtpub.com/submit-errata`, selecting your book, clicking on the Errata Submission Form link, and entering the details.

Piracy: If you come across any illegal copies of our works in any form on the internet, we would be grateful if you would provide us with the location address or website name. Please contact us at `copyright@packtpub.com` with a link to the material.

If you are interested in becoming an author: If there is a topic that you have expertise in and you are interested in either writing or contributing to a book, please visit `authors.packtpub.com`.

Reviews

Please leave a review. Once you have read and used this book, why not leave a review on the site that you purchased it from? Potential readers can then see and use your unbiased opinion to make purchase decisions, we at Packt can understand what you think about our products, and our authors can see your feedback on their book. Thank you!

For more information about Packt, please visit `packtpub.com`.

Introduction to the MERN Stack 1

In this chapter, we will cover the following topics:

- The MVC architectural pattern
- Installing and configuring MongoDB
- Installing Node.js
- Installing NPM packages

Technical requirements

You will be required to have an IDE, Visual Studio Code, Node.js and MongoDB. You will also need to install Git, in order use the Git repository of this book.

The code files of this chapter can be found on GitHub:
https://github.com/PacktPublishing/MERN-Quick-Start-Guide/tree/master/Chapter01

Check out the following video to see the code in action:
https://goo.gl/1zwc6F

Introduction

The MERN stack is a solution composed of four main components:

- **MongoDB**: A database that uses a document-oriented data model.
- **ExpressJS**: A web application framework for building web applications and APIs.
- **ReactJS**: A declarative, component-based, and isomorphic JavaScript library for building user interfaces.
- **Node.js**: A cross-platform JavaScript runtime environment built on Chrome's V8 JavaScript engine allows developers to build diverse tools, servers, and applications.

These fundamental components that comprise the MERN stack are open source, and are thus maintained and developed by a great community of developers. What ties these components together is a common language, JavaScript.

The recipes in this chapter will mainly focus on setting up a development environment to work with a MERN stack.

You are free to use the code editor or IDE of your choice. However, I would suggest you give Visual Studio Code a try if you have trouble deciding which IDE to use.

The MVC architectural pattern

Most modern web applications implement the MVC architectural pattern. It consists of three interconnected parts that separate the internal representation of information in a web application:

- **Model**: Manages the business logic of an application that determines how data should be stored, created, and modified
- **View**: Any visual representation of the data or information
- **Controller**: Interprets user-generated events and transforms them into commands for the model and view to update accordingly:

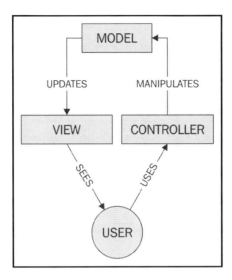

The **Separation of Concern (SoC)** design pattern separates frontend from backend code. Following the MVC architectural pattern, developers are able to adhere to the SoC design pattern, resulting in a consistent and manageable application structure.

The recipes in the following chapters implement this architectural pattern to separate the frontend and the backend.

Installing and configuring MongoDB

The official MongoDB website provides up-to-date packages containing binaries for installing MongoDB on Linux, OS X, and Windows.

Getting ready

Visit the official website of MongoDB at `https://www.mongodb.com/download-center`, select **Community Server**, and then select your preferred operating system version of the software and download it.

Installing MongoDB and configuring it may require additional steps.

How to do it...

Visit the documentation website of MongoDB at `https://docs.mongodb.com/master/installation/` for instructions and check the Tutorials section for your specific platform.

After installation, an instance of `mongod–`, the daemon process for `MongoDB–`, can be started in a standalone fashion:

1. Open a new Terminal
2. Create a new directory named `data`, which will contain the Mongo database
3. Type `mongod --port 27017 --dbpath /data/` to start a new instance and create a database
4. Open another Terminal
5. Type `mongo --port 27017` to connect a Mongo shell to the instance

There's more...

As an alternative, you can opt to use a **Database as a service (DBaaS)** such as MongoDB Atlas, which, at the time of writing, allows you to create a free cluster with 512 MB of storage. Another simple alternative is mLab, although there are many other options.

Installing Node.js

The official Node.js website provides two packages containing LTS and Current (containing the latest features) binaries to install Node.js on Linux, OS X, and Windows.

Getting ready

For the purpose of this book, we will install Node.js v10.1.x.

How to do it...

To download the latest version of Node.js:

1. Visit the official website at `https://nodejs.org/en/download/`
2. Select **Current | Latest Features**
3. Select the binary for your preferred platform or **operating system (OS)**
4. Download and install

If you prefer to install Node.js via package manager, visit `https://nodejs.org/en/download/package-manager/` and select your preferred platform or OS.

Installing npm packages

The installation of Node.js includes a package manager called `npm`, which is the default and most widely used package manager for installing JavaScript/Node.js libraries.

NPM packages are listed in the NPM registry at `https://registry.npmjs.org/`, where you can search for packages and even publish your own.

There are other alternatives to NPM as well, such as Yarn, which is compatible with the public NPM registry. You are free to use the package manager of your choice; however, for the purpose of this book, the package manager used in the recipes will be NPM.

Getting ready

NPM expects to find a `package.json` file at the root of your `project` folder. This is a configuration file that describes the details of your project, such as its dependencies, the name of the project, and the author of the project.

Before you're able to install any packages in your project, you must create a `package.json` file. These are the steps you will usually take to create a project:

1. Create a new `project` folder in your preferred location and either name it `mern-cookbook` or give it another name of your choice.
2. Open a new Terminal.
3. Change the current directory to the new folder you just created. This is usually done with the `cd` command in your Terminal.
4. Run `npm init` to create a new `package.json` file, following the steps displayed in the Terminal.

After that, you should have a `package.json` file that will look something like the following:

```
{
    "name": "mern-cookbook",
    "version": "1.0.0",
    "description": "mern cookbook recipes",
    "main": "index.js",
    "scripts": {
        "test": "echo \"Error: no test specified\" && exit 1"
    },
    "author": "Eddy Wilson",
    "license": "MIT"
}
```

After this, you will be able to use NPM to install new packages for your project.

How to do it...

1. Open a new Terminal
2. Change the current directory to where your newly created `project` folder is located
3. Run the following line to install the `chalk` package:

```
npm --save-exact install chalk
```

Now, you will be able to use the package in your project via require in Node.js. Go through the following steps to see how you can use it:

1. Create a new file named `index.js` and add the following code:

```
const chalk = require('chalk')
const { red, blue } = chalk
console.log(red('hello'), blue('world!'))
```

2. Then, open a new Terminal and run the following:

```
node index.js
```

How it works...

NPM will connect to and look in the NPM registry for the package named react, and will download it and install it if it exists.

The following are some useful flags that you can use NPM with:

- `--save`: This will install and add the package name and version in the `dependencies` section of your `package.json` file. These dependencies are modules that your project will use while in production.
- `--save-dev`: This works in the same way as the `--save` flag. It will install and add the package name in the `devDependencies` section of the `package.json` file. These dependencies are modules that your project will use during development.
- `--save-exact`: This keeps the original version of the installed package. This means, if you share your project with other people, they will be able to install the exact same version of the package that you use.

While this book will provide you with a step-by-step guide to installing the necessary packages in every recipe, you are encouraged to visit the NPM documentation website at `https://docs.npmjs.com/getting-started/using-a-package.json` to learn more.

Building a Web server with ExpressJS 2

In this chapter, we will cover the following recipes:

- Routing in ExpressJS
- Modular route handlers
- Writing middleware functions
- Writing configurable middleware functions
- Writing router-level middleware functions
- Writing error-handler middleware functions
- Using ExpressJS' built-in middleware function to serve static assets
- Parsing the HTTP request body
- Compressing HTTP responses
- Using an HTTP request logger
- Managing and creating virtual domains
- Securing an ExpressJS web application with helmet
- Using template engines
- Debugging your ExpressJS web application

Technical requirements

You will be required to have an IDE, Visual Studio Code, Node.js and MongoDB. You will also need to install Git, in order use the Git repository of this book.

The code files of this chapter can be found on GitHub:
`https://github.com/PacktPublishing/MERN-Quick-Start-Guide/tree/master/Chapter02`

Check out the following video to see the code in action:
`https://goo.gl/xXhqWK`

Introduction

ExpressJS is the preferred de facto Node.js web application framework for building robust web applications and APIs.

In this chapter, the recipes will focus on building a fully functional web server and understanding the core fundamentals.

Routing in ExpressJS

Routing refers to how an application responds or acts when a resource is requested via an HTTP verb or HTTP method.

HTTP stands for **Hypertext Transfer Protocol** and it's the basis of data communication for the **World Wide Web (WWW)**. All documents and data in the WWW are identified by a **Uniform Resource Locator (URL)**.

HTTP verbs or HTTP methods are a *client-server* model. Typically, a web browser serves as a *client*, and in our case ExpressJS is the framework that allows us to create a *server* capable of understanding these requests. Every request expects a response to be sent to the client to recognize the status of the resource that it is requesting.

Request methods can be:

- **Safe**: An HTTP verb that performs read-only operations on the server. In other words, it does not alter the server state. For example: GET.
- **Idempotent**: An HTTP verb that has the same effect on the server when identical requests are made. For instance, sending a PUT request to modify a user's first name should have the same effect on the server if implemented correctly when multiple identical requests are sent. All *safe* methods are also idempotent. For example, the GET, PUT, and DELETE methods are idempotent.
- **Cacheable**: An HTTP response that can be cached. Not all methods or HTTP verbs can be cached. A response is cacheable only if the *status code* of the response and the method used to make the request are both cacheable. For example, the GET method is cacheable and the following status codes: 200 (Request succeeded), 204 (No content), 206 (Partial content), 301 (Moved permanently), 404 (Not found), 405 (Method not allowed), 410 (Gone or Content permanently removed from server), and 414 (URI too long).

Getting ready

Understanding routing is one of the most important core aspects in building robust RESTful APIs.

In this recipe, we will see how ExpressJS handles or interprets HTTP requests. Before you start, create a new package.json file with the following content:

```
{
    "dependencies": {
        "express": "4.16.3"
    }
}
```

Then, install the dependencies by opening a Terminal and running:

```
npm install
```

ExpressJS does the whole job of understanding a client's request. The request may come from a browser, for instance. Once the request has been interpreted, ExpressJS saves all the information in two objects:

- **Request**: This contains all the data and information about the client's request. For instance, ExpressJS parses the URI and makes its parameters available on request.query.
- **Response**: This contains data and information that will be sent to the client. The response's headers can be modified as well before sending the information to the client. The `response` object has several methods available for sending the status code and data to the client. For instance: `response.status(200).send('Some Data!')`.

How to do it...

`Request` and `Response` objects are passed as arguments to the *route handlers* defined inside a `route` method.

Route methods

These are derived from HTTP verbs or HTTP methods. A route method is used to define the response that an application will have for a specific HTTP verb.

ExpressJS route methods have equivalent names to HTTP verbs. For instance: `app.get()` for the GET HTTP verb or `app.delete()` for the DELETE HTTP verb.

A very basic route can be written as the following:

1. Create a new file named `1-basic-route.js`
2. Include the ExpressJS library first and initialize a new ExpressJS application:

```
const express = require('express')
const app = express()
```

3. Add a new route method to handle requests for the path `"/"`. The first argument specifies the path or URL, the next argument is the route handler. Inside the route handler, let's use the `response` object to send a status code `200` `(OK)` and text to the client:

```
app.get('/', (request, response, nextHandler) => {
    response.status(200).send('Hello from ExpressJS')
})
```

4. Finally, use the `listen` method to accept new connections on port `1337`:

```
app.listen(
    1337,
        () => console.log('Web Server running on port 1337'),
)
```

5. Save the file
6. Open a Terminal and run the following command:

```
node 1-basic-route.js
```

7. Open a new tab on your browser and visit `localhost` on port `1337` in your web browser to see the results:

```
http://localhost:1337/
```

 For more information about which HTTP methods are supported by ExpressJS, visit the official ExpressJS website at `https://expressjs.com/en/guide/routing.html#route-methods`.

Route handlers

Route handlers are callback functions that accept three arguments. The first one is the request object, the second one is the response object, and the last one is a callback, which passes the handler to the next request handler in the chain. Multiple callback functions can be used inside a route method as well.

Let's see a working example of how we could write route handlers inside route methods:

1. Create a new file named 2-route-handlers.js

2. Include the ExpressJS library, then initialize a new ExpressJS application:

```
const express = require('express')
const app = express()
```

3. Add two route methods to handle a request in the same path "/one". Use the type method of the response object to set the content type of the response sent to the client to text/plain. Using the write method send partial data to the client. To finalize sending data, use the end method of the response object. Calling nextHandler will pass the handler to the second handler in the chain:

```
app.get('/one', (request, response, nextHandler) => {
    response.type('text/plain')
    response.write('Hello ')
    nextHandler()
})
app.get('/one', (request, response, nextHandler) => {
    response.status(200).end('World!')
})
```

4. Add a route method to handle a request in the path "/two". Two route handlers are defined inside the route method to handle the same request:

```
app.get('/two',
    (request, response, nextHandler) => {
        response.type('text/plain')
        response.write('Hello ')
        nextHandler()
    },
    (request, response, nextHandler) => {
        response.status(200).end('Moon!')
    }
)
```

5. Use the `listen` method to accept new connections on port `1337`:

```
app.listen(
    1337,
    () => console.log('Web Server running on port 1337'),
)
```

6. Save the file
7. Open a Terminal and run:

```
node 2-route-handlers.js
```

8. To see the result, open a new tab in your web browser and visit:

```
http://localhost:1337/one
http://localhost:1337/two
```

Chainable route methods

Route methods can be chainable using `app.route(path)` because the `path` is specified for a single location. This is probably the best approach when dealing with multiple route methods because, besides making the code more readable and less prone to typos and redundancy, it allows to work with multiple route methods at the same time.

1. Create a new file named `3-chainable-routes.js`
2. Initialize a new ExpressJS application:

```
const express = require('express')
const app = express()
```

3. Chain three route methods using the `route` method:

```
app
.route('/home')
.get((request, response, nextHandler) => {
    response.type('text/html')
    response.write('<!DOCTYPE html>')
    nextHandler()
})
.get((request, response, nextHandler) => {
    response.end(`
    <html lang="en">
        <head>
        <meta charset="utf-8">
        <title>WebApp powered by ExpressJS</title>
```

```
        </head>
        <body role="application">
            <form method="post" action="/home">
                <input type="text" />
                <button type="submit">Send</button>
            </form>
        </body>
    </html>
    `)
})
.post((request, response, nextHandler) => {
    response.send('Got it!')
})
```

4. Use the `listen` method to accept new connections on port 1337:

```
app.listen(
    1337,
    () => console.log('Web Server running on port 1337'),
)
```

5. Save the file
6. Open a terminal and run:

   node 3-chainable-routes.js

7. To see the result, open a new tab in your web browser and visit:

   `http://localhost:1337/home`

There's more...

Route paths can be strings or regular expressions. Route paths are internally turned into regular expressions using the `path-to-regexp` NPM package `https://www.npmjs.com/package/path-to-regexp`.

`path-to-regexp`, in a way, helps you write path regular expressions in a more human-readable way. For example, consider the following code:

```
app.get(/([a-z]+)-([0-9]+)$/, (request, response, nextHandler) => {
    response.send(request.params)
})
// Output: {"0":"abc","1":"12345"} for path /abc-12345
```

This could be written as follows:

```
app.get('/:0-:1', (request, response, nextHandler) => {
    response.send(request.params)
})
// Outputs: {"0":"abc","1":"12345"} for /abc-12345
```

Or better:

```
app.get('/:id-:tag', (request, response, nextHandler) => {
    response.send(request.params)
})
// Outputs: {"id":"abc","tag":"12345"} for /abc-12345
```

Take a look at this expression: `/([a-z]+)-([0-9]+)$/`. The parentheses in the regular expression are called **capturing parentheses**; and when they find a match, they remember it. In the preceding example, for `abc-12345`, two strings are remembered, `{"0":"abc","1":"12345"}`. This is the way that ExpressJS finds a match, remembers its value, and associates it to a key:

```
app.get('/:userId/:action-:where', (request, response, nextHandler) => {
    response.send(request.params)
})
// Route path: /123/edit-profile
// Outputs: {"userId":"123","action":"edit","where":"profile"}
```

Modular route handlers

ExpressJS has a built-in class called **router**. A router is just a class that allows developers to write mountable and modular route handlers.

A **Router** is an instance of ExpressJS' core routing system. That means, all routing methods from an ExpressJS application are available:

```
const router = express.Router()
router.get('/', (request, response, next) => {
  response.send('Hello there!')
})
router.post('/', (request, response, next) => {
  response.send('I got your data!')
})
```

Getting ready

In this recipe, we will see how to use a router to make a modular application. Before you start, create a new `package.json` file with the following content:

```
{
    "dependencies": {
        "express": "4.16.3"
    }
}
```

Then, install the dependencies by opening a terminal and running:

```
npm install
```

How to do it...

Suppose that you want to write a modular mini-application within your ExpressJS main application that can be mounted to any URI. You want to be able to choose the path where to mount it, or you just want to mount the same route methods and handlers to several others paths or a URI.

1. Create a new file named `modular-router.js`
2. Initialize a new ExpressJS application:

```
const express = require('express')
const app = express()
```

3. Define a router for your mini-application and add a request method to handle requests for path `"/home"`:

```
const miniapp = express.Router()
miniapp.get('/home', (request, response, next) => {
    const url = request.originalUrl
    response
        .status(200)
        .send(`You are visiting /home from ${url}`)
})
```

4. Mount your modular mini-application to `"/first"` path, and to `"/second"` path:

```
app.use('/first', miniapp)
app.use('/second', miniapp)
```

5. Listen for new connections on port 1337:

```
app.listen(
    1337,
    () => console.log('Web Server running on port 1337'),
)
```

6. Save the file
7. Open a Terminal and run the following command:

```
node modular-router.js
```

8. To see the results, navigate in your web browser to:

```
http://localhost:1337/first/home
http://localhost:1337/second/home
```

You will see two different outputs:

```
You are visting /home from /first/home
You are visting /home from /second/home
```

As can be seen, a *router* was mounted to two different mount points. Routers are usually referred to as mini-applications because they can be mounted to an ExpressJS application's specific routes and not only once but also several times to different mount points, paths, or URIs.

Writing middleware functions

Middleware functions are mainly used to make changes in the request and response object. They are executed in sequence, one after another, but if a middleware functions does not pass control to the next one, the request is left hanging.

Getting ready

Middleware functions have the following signature:

```
app.use((request, response, next) => {
    next()
})
```

The signature is very similar to writing route handlers. In fact, a middleware function can be written for a specific HTTP method and a specific path route, and will look like this, for example:

```
app.get('/', (request, response, next) => {
    next()
})
```

So, if you are wondering what the difference is between route handlers, and middleware functions, the answer is simple: their purpose.

If you are writing route handlers, and the `request` objects and/or the `response` object is modified, then you are writing middleware functions.

In this recipe, you will see how to use a middleware function to restrict access to certain paths or routes that depend on a certain condition. Before you start, create a new `package.json` file with the following content:

```
{
    "dependencies": {
        "express": "4.16.3"
    }
}
```

Then, install the dependencies by opening a terminal and running:

```
npm install
```

How to do it...

We will write a middleware function that allows access to the root path `"/"` only when the query parameter `allowme` is present:

1. Create a new file named `middleware-functions.js`
2. Initialize a new ExpressJS application:

```
const express = require('express')
const app = express()
```

3. Write a middleware function that will add a property `allowed` to the `request` object:

```
app.use((request, response, next) => {
    request.allowed = Reflect.has(request.query, 'allowme')
    next()
})
```

4. Add a request method to handle requests for path "`/`":

```
app.get('/', (request, response, next) => {
    if (request.allowed) {
        response.send('Hello secret world!')
    } else {
        response.send('You are not allowed to enter')
    }
})
```

5. Listen on port `1337` for new connections:

```
app.listen(
    1337,
    () => console.log('Web Server running on port 1337'),
)
```

6. Save the file

7. Open a terminal and run:

`node middleware-functions.js`

8. To see the results, in your web browser, navigate to:

```
http://localhost:1337/
http://localhost:1337/?allowme
```

How it works...

Just like with route handlers, middleware functions need to pass control to the next handler; otherwise, our application will have been hanging because no data was sent to the client, and the connection was not closed either.

If new properties are added to the `request` or `response` objects inside a middleware function, the next handler will have access to those new properties. As in our previously written code, the `allowed property` in the `request` object is available to the next handler.

Writing configurable middleware functions

A common pattern for writing middleware functions is to wrap the middleware function inside another function. The result of doing so is a configurable middleware function. They are also *higher-order functions*, that is, a function that returns another function.

```
const fn = (options) => (response, request, next) => {
    next()
}
```

Usually an object is used as an `options` parameters. However, there is nothing stopping you from doing it in your own way.

Getting ready

In this recipe, you will write a configurable logger middleware function. Before you start, create a new `package.json` file with the following content:

```
{
    "dependencies": {
        "express": "4.16.3"
    }
}
```

Then, install the dependencies by opening a terminal and running:

```
npm install
```

How to do it...

What your configurable middleware function will do is simple: it will print the status code and the URL when a request is made.

1. Create a new file named `middleware-logger.js`

2. Export a function that accepts an object as the first argument. The function expects the object to have a property `enable`, which can be either `true` or `false`:

```
const logger = (options) => (request, response, next) => {
    if (typeof options === 'object'
        && options !== null
        && options.enable) {
        console.log(
            'Status Code:', response.statusCode,
            'URL:', request.originalUrl,
        )
    }
    next()
}
module.exports = logger
```

3. Save the file

Let's test it...

Our configurable middleware function is not useful on its own. Create a simple ExpressJS application to see our middleware actually working:

1. Create a new file named `configurable-middleware-test.js`
2. Include our `middleware-logger.js` module and initialize a new ExpressJS application:

```
const express = require('express')
const loggerMiddleware = require('./middleware-logger')
const app = express()
```

3. Use the `use` method to include our configurable middleware function. When the `enable` property is set to `true`, your logger will work and log every request's status code and URL to the terminal:

```
app.use(loggerMiddleware({
    enable: true,
}))
```

4. Listen on port `1337` for new connections:

```
app.listen(
    1337,
    () => console.log('Web Server running on port 1337'),
)
```

5. Save the file
6. Open a terminal and run:

`node middleware-logger-test.js`

7. In your browser, navigate to:

`http://localhost:1337/hello?world`

8. The Terminal should display:

`Status Code: 200 URL: /hello?world`

There's more...

If you want to experiment, start your configurable middleware test application with the `enable` property set to `false`. No logs should be displayed.

Usually, you would want to disable logging in production, since this operation could hit performance.

An alternative to disabling all logging is to use other libraries to do this task instead of using `console`. There are libraries that allow you to set different levels of logging as well, for instance:

- **Debug module**: `https://www.npmjs.com/package/debug`
- **Winston**: `https://www.npmjs.com/package/winston`

Logging is useful for several reasons. The main reasons are:

- It checks whether your services are running properly, for example, checking whether your application is connected to MongoDB.
- It discovers errors and bugs.
- It helps you to understand better how your application is working. For instance, if you have a modular application, you can see how it integrates when included in other applications.

Writing router-level middleware functions

Router-level middleware functions are only executed inside a router. They are usually used when applying a middleware to a mount point only or to a specific path.

Getting ready

In this recipe, you will create a small logger router-level middleware function that will only log requests to paths mounted or located in the router's mounted path. Before you start, create a new `package.json` file with the following content:

```
{
    "dependencies": {
        "express": "4.16.3"
    }
}
```

Then, install the dependencies by opening a Terminal and running:

```
npm install
```

How to do it...

1. Create a new file named `router-level.js`
2. Initialize a new ExpressJS application and define a router:

```
const express = require('express')
const app = express()
const router = express.Router()
```

3. Define our logger middleware function:

```
router.use((request, response, next) => {
    console.log('URL:', request.originalUrl)
    next()
})
```

4. Mount the Router to the path "`/router`"

```
app.use('/router', router)
```

5. Listen on port `1337` for new connections:

```
app.listen(
    1337,
    () => console.log('Web Server running on port 1337'),
)
```

6. Save the file

7. Open a terminal and run:

`node router-level.js`

8. In your web browser navigate to:

`http://localhost:1337/router/example`

9. The Terminal should display:

`URL: /router/example`

10. After, in your web browser, navigate to:

```
http://localhost:1337/example
```

11. No logs should be displayed in terminal

There's more...

It is possible to pass control back to the next middleware function or route method outside of a router by calling `next('router')`.

```
router.use((request, response, next) => {
  next('route')
})
```

For example, by creating a router that expects to receive a user ID as a query parameter. The `next('router')` function can be used to get out of the router or pass control to the next middleware function outside of the router when a user ID is not provided. The next middleware function out of the router can be used to display other information when the router passes control to it. For example:

1. Create a new file named `router-level-control.js`
2. Initialize a new ExpressJS application:

```
const express = require('express')
const app = express()
```

3. Define a new router:

```
const router = express.Router()
```

4. Define our logger middleware function inside the router:

```
router.use((request, response, next) => {
    if (!request.query.id) {
        next('router') // Next, out of Router
    } else {
      next() // Next, in Router
    }
})
```

5. Add a route method to handle GET requests for path "/" which will be executed only if the middleware function passes control to it:

```
router.get('/', (request, response, next) => {
    const id = request.query.id
    response.send(`You specified a user ID => ${id}`)
})
```

6. Add a route method to handle GET requests for path "/" outside of the router. However, include the router as a route handler as the second argument, and another route handler to handle the same request only if the router passes control to it:

```
app.get('/', router, (request, response, next) => {
    response
      .status(400)
      .send('A user ID needs to be specified')
})
```

7. Listen on port 1337 for new connections:

```
app.listen(
    1337,
    () => console.log('Web Server running on port 1337'),
)
```

8. Save the file

9. Open a terminal and run:

node router-level-control.js

10. To see the result, in your browser, navigate to:

```
http://localhost:1337/
http://localhost:1337/?id=7331
```

How it works...

When navigating to the first URL (http://localhost:1337/), the following message is shown:

```
A user ID needs to be specified
```

This is because the middleware function in the router checks if the id was provided in the query, and because it is not, it passes control to the next handler outside of the router with next('router').

On the other hand, when navigating to the second URL (http://localhost:1337/?id=7331), the following message is shown:

```
You specified a user ID => 7331
```

That happens because, as an id was provided in the query, the middleware function in the router will pass control to the next handler inside the router with next().

Writing error-handler middleware functions

ExpressJS already includes by default a built-in error handler which gets executed at the end of all middleware and route handlers.

There are ways that the built-in error handler can be triggered. One is implicit when an error occurs inside a route handler. For example:

```
app.get('/', (request, response, next) => {
    throw new Error('Oh no!, something went wrong!')
})
```

And another way of triggering the built-in error handler is explicit when passing an error as an argument to next(error). For instance:

```
app.get('/', (request, response, next) => {
    try {
        throw new Error('Oh no!, something went wrong!')
    } catch (error) {
        next(error)
    }
})
```

 The stack trace is displayed on the client side. If NODE_ENV is set to production, then the stack trace is not included.

A custom error handler middleware function can be written as well and it looks pretty much the same as route handlers do with the exception that an error handler function middleware expects to receive four arguments:

```
app.use((error, request, response, next) => {
    next(error)
})
```

Take into account that next(error) is optional. That means, if specified, next(error) will pass control over to the next error handler. If no other error handler was defined, then the control will pass to the built-in error handler.

Getting ready

In this recipe, we will see how to create a custom error handler. Before you start, create a new `package.json` file with the following content:

```
{
    "dependencies": {
        "express": "4.16.3"
    }
}
```

Then, install the dependencies by opening a terminal and running:

```
npm install
```

How to do it...

You will build a custom error handler that sends to the client the error message.

1. Create a new file named `custom-error-handler.js`

2. Include the ExpressJS library, then initialize a new ExpressJS application:

```
const express = require('express')
const app = express()
```

3. Define a new Route Method to handle GET requests for path `"/"` and throw an error every time:

```
app.get('/', (request, response, next) => {
    try {
        throw new Error('Oh no!, something went wrong!')
    } catch (err) {
        next(err)
    }
})
```

4. Define a custom error handler middleware function to send the error message back to the client's browser:

```
app.use((error, request, response, next) => {
    response.end(error.message)
})
```

5. Listen on port 1337 for new connections:

```
app.listen(
    1337,
    () => console.log('Web Server running on port 1337'),
)
```

6. Save the file
7. Open a terminal and run:

   node custom-error-handler.js

8. To see the result, in your web browser, navigate to:

   `http://localhost:1337/`

Using ExpressJS' built-in middleware function for serving static assets

Prior to the 4.x version of ExpressJS, it has depended on ConnectJS which is an HTTP server framework `https://github.com/senchalabs/connect`. In fact, most middleware written for ConnectJS is also supported in ExpressJS.

As from the 4.x version of ExpressJS, it no longer depends on ConnectJS, and all previously built-in middleware functions were moved to separate modules `https://expressjs.com/en/resources/middleware.html`.

ExpressJS 4.x and newer versions include only two built-in middleware functions. The first one has already been seen: the built-in error handler middleware function. The second one is the `express.static` middleware function that is responsible for serving static assets.

The `express.static` middleware function is based on `serve-static` module `https://expressjs.com/en/resources/middleware/serve-static.html`.

The main difference between `express.static` and `serve-static` is that the second one can be used outside of ExpressJS.

Getting ready

In this recipe, you will see how to build a web application that will serve static assets in a certain path. Before you start, create a new `package.json` file with the following content:

```
{
    "dependencies": {
        "express": "4.16.3"
    }
}
```

Then, install the dependencies by opening a terminal and running:

```
npm install
```

How to do it...

1. Create a new directory named `public`
2. Move into the new `public` directory
3. Create a new file named `index.html`
4. Add the following code:

```
<!DOCTYPE html>
<html lang="en">
<head>
    <meta charset="utf-8">
    <title>Simple Web Application</title>
</head>
<body>
    <section role="application">
  <h1>Welcome Home!</h1>
    </section>
</body>
</html>
```

5. Save the file
6. Navigate back out of the `public` directory
7. Create a new file named `serve-static-assets.js`

8. Add the following code. Initialize a new ExpressJS application:

```
const express = require('express')
const path = require('path')
const app = express()
```

9. Include the `express.static` configurable middleware function and Pass the path of the `/public` directory where `index.html` file is located:

```
const publicDir = path.join(__dirname, './public')
app.use('/', express.static(publicDir))
```

10. Listen on port `1337` for new connections:

```
app.listen(
    1337,
    () => console.log('Web Server running on port 1337'),
)
```

11. Save the file
12. Open a terminal and run:

    node serve-static-assets.js

13. To see the result, in your browser, navigate to:

    ```
    http://localhost:1337/index.html
    ```

How it works...

Our `index.html` file will be shown because we specified `"/"` as the root directory where to look for assets.

Try changing the path from `"/"` to `"/public"`. Then, you will be able to see that the `index.html` file, and other files that you want to include in the `/public` directory, will be accessible under `http://localhost:1337/public/[fileName]`.

There's more...

Let's pretend that you have a big project that serves dozens of static files, including images, font files, and PDF documents (those about privacy and legal stuff) among others. You decided that you want to keep them in separate files, but you do not want to change the mount path or URI. They can be served under `/public`, for example, but they will exist in separate directories in your project directory:

First, let's create the first `public` directory that will contain a single file named `index.html`:

1. Create a new directory named `public` if you didn't create it in the previous recipe
2. Move into the new `public` directory
3. Create a new file named `index.html`
4. Add the following code:

```
<!DOCTYPE html>
<html lang="en">
<head>
    <meta charset="utf-8">
    <title>Simple Web Application</title>
</head>
<body>
    <section role="application">
    <h1>Welcome Home!</h1>
    </section>
</body>
</html>
```

5. Save the file

Now, let's create a second public directory that will contain another file named `second.html`:

6. Move back out of the `public` directory
7. Create a new directory named `another-public`
8. Move into the new `another-public` directory
9. Create a new empty file named `second.html`

10. Add the following code:

```
<!DOCTYPE html>
<html lang="en">
<head>
    <meta charset="utf-8">
    <title>Simple Web Application</title>
</head>
<body>
    <section role="application">
     Welcome to Second Page!
    </section>
</body>
 </html>
```

11. Save the file

As you can see, both files exist in different directories. To serve those files under one mount point:

1. Move back out of the `another-public` directory
2. Create a new file named `router-serve-static.js`
3. Include the ExpressJS and path libraries. Then, initialize a new ExpressJS application:

```
const express = require('express')
const path = require('path')
const app = express()
```

4. Define a router:

```
const staticRouter = express.Router()
```

5. Use the `express.static` configurable middleware function to include both directories, `public` and `another-public`:

```
const assets = {
    first: path.join(__dirname, './public'),
    second: path.join(__dirname, './another-public')
}
 staticRouter
    .use(express.static(assets.first))
    .use(express.static(assets.second))
```

6. Mount the Router to the "/" path:

```
app.use('/', staticRouter)
```

7. Listen on port 1337 for new connections:

```
app.listen(
    1337,
        () => console.log('Web Server running on port 1337'),
    )
```

8. Save the file
9. Open a terminal and run:

node router-serve-static.js

10. To see the result, in the browser, navigate to:

```
http://localhost:1337/index.html
http://localhost:1337/second.html
```

11. Two different files in different locations were served under one path

 If two or more files with the same name exist under different directories, only the first one found will be displayed on the client-side.

Parsing the HTTP request body

`body-parser` is a middleware function that parses the incoming request body and makes it available in the `request` object as
`request.body` https://expressjs.com/en/resources/middleware/body-parser.html.

This module allows an application to parse the incoming request as:

- JSON
- Text
- Raw (buffer original incoming data)
- URL encoded form

The module supports automatic decompression of gzip and deflates encodings when the incoming request is compressed.

Getting ready

In this recipe, you will see how to use the `body-parser` NPM module to parse the content body sent from two different forms encoded in two different ways. Before you start, create a new `package.json` file with the following content:

```
{
    "dependencies": {
        "body-parser": "1.18.2",
        "express": "4.16.3"
    }
}
```

Then, install the dependencies by opening a terminal and running:

```
npm install
```

How to do it...

Two forms will be displayed to the user, both of them will send data to our web server application encoded in two different ways. The first one is a URL encoded form while the other one will encode its body as plain text.

1. Create a file named `parse-form.js`
2. Include the `body-parser` NPM module. Then, initialize a new ExpressJS application:

   ```
   const express = require('express')
   const bodyParser = require('body-parser')
   const app = express()
   ```

3. Include the `body-parser` middleware functions to handle URL encoded requests and text plain requests:

   ```
   app.use(bodyParser.urlencoded({ extended: true }))
   app.use(bodyParser.text())
   ```

4. Add a new route method to handle GET requests for path `"/"`. Serve HTML content with two forms that submit data using different encodings:

   ```
   app.get('/', (request, response, next) => {
       response.send(`
       <!DOCTYPE html>
       <html lang="en">
   ```

```
    <head>
      <meta charset="utf-8">
      <title>WebApp powered by ExpressJS</title>
    </head>
  <body>
    <div role="application">
      <form method="post" action="/setdata">
          <input name="urlencoded" type="text" />
          <button type="submit">Send</button>
      </form>
      <form method="post" action="/setdata"
        enctype="text/plain">
        <input name="txtencoded" type="text" />
        <button type="submit">Send</button>
      </form>
    </div>
  </body>
  </html>
  `)
})
```

5. Add a new route method to handle POST requests for path "/setdata". Display on terminal the content of request.body:

```
app.post('/setdata', (request, response, next) => {
    console.log(request.body)
    response.end()
})
```

6. Listen on port 1337 for new connections:

```
app.listen(
    1337,
    () => console.log('Web Server running on port 1337'),
)
```

7. Save the file

8. Open a terminal and run:

node parse-form.js

9. In your web browser, navigate to:

http://localhost:1337/

10. Fill the first input box with any data and submit the form:
11. In your web browser, navigate back to:

```
http://localhost:1337/
```

12. Fill the second input box with any data and submit the form:
13. Check the output in the terminal

How it works...

Terminal outputs something like:

```
{ 'urlencoded': 'Example' }
txtencoded=Example
```

Two parsers are used above:

1. The first one `bodyParser.urlencoded()` parses incoming requests for `multipart/form-data` encoding type. The result is available as an **Object** in `request.body`
2. The second one `bodyParser.text()` parses incoming requests for `text/plain` encoding type. The result is available as a **String** in `request.body`

Compressing HTTP responses

compression is a middleware function that compresses the response body that will be send to the client. This module uses the `zlib` module `https://nodejs.org/api/zlib.html` that supports the following content-encoding mechanisms:

- gzip
- deflate

The `Accept-Encoding` HTTP header is used to determine which content-encoding mechanism is supported on the client-side (for example web browser) while the `Content-Encoding` HTTP header is used to tell the client which content encoding mechanism was applied to the response body.

compression is a configurable middleware function. It accepts an options object as the first argument to define a specific behavior for the middleware and also to pass zlib options as well.

Getting ready

In this recipe, we will see how to configure and use the compression NPM module to compress the request body sent to the client. Before you start, create a new package.json file with the following content:

```
{
    "dependencies": {
        "compression": "1.7.2",
        "express": "4.16.3"
    }
}
```

Then, install the dependencies by opening a terminal and running:

```
npm install
```

How to do it...

1. Create a new file named compress-site.js
2. Include the compression NPM module. Then, initialize a new ExpressJS application:

```
const express = require('express')
const compression = require('compression')
const app = express()
```

3. Include the compression middleware function. Specify the level of compression to 9 (best compression) and threshold, or minimum size in bytes that the response should have to consider compressing the response body, to 0 bytes:

```
app.use(compression({ level: 9, threshold: 0 }))
```

4. Define a route method to handle GET requests for path "/" which will serve a sample HTML content that we expect to be compressed and will print the encodings that the client accepts:

```
app.get('/', (request, response, next) => {
    response.send(`
    <!DOCTYPE html>
    <html lang="en">
    <head>
        <meta charset="utf-8">
        <title>WebApp powered by ExpressJS</title>
    </head>
    <body>
        <section role="application">
            <h1>Hello! this page is compressed!</h1>
        </section>
    </body>
    </html>
    `)
    console.log(request.acceptsEncodings())
})
```

5. Listen on port 1337 for new connections:

```
app.listen(
    1337,
    () => console.log('Web Server running on port 1337'),
)
```

6. Save the file
7. Open a terminal and run:

   node compress-site.js

8. In your browser, navigate to:

   ```
   http://localhost:1337/
   ```

How it works...

The output of the Terminal will show the content encoding mechanism that the client (for example web browser) supports. It may look something like this:

```
[ 'gzip', 'deflate', 'sdch', 'br', 'identity' ]
```

The content encoding mechanism sent by the client is used by `compression` internally to know if compression is supported. If compression is not supported, then the response body is not compressed.

If opening Chrome Dev Tools or similar and analyzing the request made, the `Content-Encoding` header that was sent by the server indicates the kind of content encoding mechanism used by `compression`.

▼ Response Headers   view source
   Connection: keep-alive
   Content-Encoding: gzip
   Content-Type: text/html; charset=utf-8

Chrome Dev Tools | Network Tab displaying Response Headers

The `compression` library sets the `Content-Encoding` header to the encoding mechanism used for compressing the response body.

The `threshold` option is set by default to 1 KB which means that if the response size is below the number of bytes specified, then it is not compressed. Set it to 0 or `false` to compress the response even when the size is below 1 KB

Using an HTTP request logger

As previously seen, writing a request logger is simple. However, writing our own could take precious time. Luckily, there are several other alternatives out there. For example, a very popular HTTP request logger widely used is morgan https://expressjs.com/en/resources/middleware/morgan.html.

morgan is a configurable middleware function that takes two arguments `format` and `options` which are used to specify the format in which the logs are displayed and what kind of information needs to be displayed.

There are several predefined formats:

- `tiny`: Minimal output
- `short`: Same as tiny, including remote IP address
- `common`: Standard Apache log output
- `combined`: Standard Apache combined log output
- `dev`: Displays the same information as the tiny format does. However, the response statuses are colored.

Getting ready

Create a new `package.json` file with the following content:

```
{
    "dependencies": {
        "express": "4.16.3",
        "morgan": "1.9.0"
    }
}
```

Then, install the dependencies by opening a terminal and running:

```
npm install
```

How to do it...

Let's build a working example. We will include the **morgan** configurable middleware function with the `dev` format to display information of every request.

1. Create a new file named `morgan-logger.js`
2. Initialize a new ExpressJS application:

```
const express = require('express')
const morgan = require('morgan')
const app = express()
```

3. Include the `morgan` configurable middleware. Pass `'dev'` as the format we will use as the first argument to the middleware function:

```
app.use(morgan('dev'))
```

4. Define a route method to handle all GET requests:

```
app.get('*', (request, response, next) => {
    response.send('Hello Morgan!')
})
```

5. Listen on port `1337` for new connections:

```
app.listen(
    1337,
    () => console.log('Web Server running on port 1337'),
)
```

6. Save the file
7. Open a terminal and run:

   node morgan-logger.js

8. To see the result in your terminal, in your web browser, navigate to:

```
http://localhost:1337/
http://localhost:1337/example
```

Managing and creating virtual domains

Managing virtual domains is really easy with ExpressJS. Imagine that you have two or more subdomains, and you want to serve two different web applications. However, you do not want to create a different web server application for each subdomain. In this kind of situation, ExpressJS allows developers to manage virtual domains within a single web server application using **vhost** https://expressjs.com/en/resources/middleware/vhost.html.

vhost is a configurable middleware function that accepts two arguments. The first one is the `hostname`. The second argument is the request handler which will be called when the `hostname` matches.

The `hostname` follows the same rules as route paths do. They can be either a string or a regular expression.

Getting ready

Create a new `package.json` file with the following content:

```
{
    "dependencies": {
        "express": "4.16.3",
        "vhost": "3.0.2"
    }
}
```

Then, install the dependencies by opening a terminal and running:

```
npm install
```

How to do it...

Build two mini applications using **Router** that will be served in two different sub-domains:

1. Create a new file named `virtual-domains.js`
2. Include `vhost` NPM module. Then, initialize a new ExpressJS application:

```
const express = require('express')
const vhost = require('vhost')
const app = express()
```

3. Define two routers that we will use to build two mini-applications:

```
const app1 = express.Router()
const app2 = express.Router()
```

4. Add a route method to handle GET requests for path "/" in the first router:

```
app1.get('/', (request, response, next) => {
  response.send('This is the main application.')
})
```

5. Add a route method to handle GET requests for path "/" in the second router:

```
app2.get('/', (request, response, next) => {
    response.send('This is a second application.')
})
```

6. Mount our routers to our ExpressJS application. Serve the first application under localhost and the second under second.localhost:

```
app.use(vhost('localhost', app1))
app.use(vhost('second.localhost', app2))
```

7. Listen on port 1337 for new connections:

```
app.listen(
    1337,
        () => console.log('Web Server running on port 1337'),
)
```

8. Save the file

9. Open a terminal and run:

```
node virtual-domains.js
```

10. To see the result, in your web browser navigate to:

```
http://localhost:1337/
http://second.localhost:1337/
```

There's more...

vhost adds a vhost object to the request object, which contains the complete hostname (displaying the hostname and port), hostname (without the port), and matching strings. These give you more control in how to handle virtual domains.

For example, we could write an application that allows users to have their own sub-domain with their name:

1. Create a new file named user-subdomains.js

2. Include the vhost NPM module. Then, initialize a new ExpressJS application:

```
const express = require('express')
const vhost = require('vhost')
const app = express()
```

3. Define a new router. Then, add a route method to handle GET requests on path "/". Use the vhost object to access the array of subdomains:

```
const users = express.Router()
users.get('/', (request, response, next) => {
  const username = request
      .vhost[0]
      .split('-')
      .map(name => (
          name[0].toUpperCase() +
          name.slice(1)
      ))
      .join(' ')
  response.send(`Hello, ${username}`)
})
```

4. Mount the router:

```
app.use(vhost('*.localhost', users))
```

5. Listen on port 1337 for new connections:

```
app.listen(
    1337,
    () => console.log('Web Server running on port 1337'),
)
```

6. Save the file
7. Open a terminal and run:

```
node user-subdomains.js
```

8. To see the result, in your web browser, navigate to:

```
http://john-smith.localhost:1337/
http://jx-huang.localhost:1337/
http://batman.localhost:1337/
```

an ExpressJS web application with

...ect web server applications against common attacks, such as **cross-**
...soi, insecure requests, and clickjacking.

Helmet is a collection of 12 middleware functions that allow you to set specific HTTP headers:

1. `Content Security Policy (CSP)`: This is an effective way to whitelist what kind of external resources are allowed in your web application, such as JavaScript, CSS, and images, for instance.
2. `Certificate Transparency`: This is a way of providing more transparency for certificates issued for a specific domain or specific domains `https://sites.google.com/a/chromium.org/dev/Home/chromium-security/certificate-transparency`.
3. `DNS Prefetch Control`: This tells the browser if it should perform domain name resolution (DNS) on resources that are not yet loaded, such as links.
4. `Frameguard`: This helps to prevent **clickjacking** by telling the browser not to allow your web application to be put inside an `iframe`.
5. `Hide Powered-By`: This simply hides the `X-Powered-By` header indicates not to display what technology powers the server. ExpressJS sets this header to `"Express"` by default.
6. `HTTP Public Key Pinning`: This helps to prevent **man-in-the-middle-attacks** by pinning your web application's public keys to the `Public-Key-Pins`header.
7. `HTTP Strict Transport Security`: This tells the browser to strictly stick to the HTTPs version of your web application.
8. `IE No Open`: This prevents Internet Explorer from executing untrusted downloads, or HTML files, on the context of your site, thus preventing the injection of malicious scripts.
9. `No Cache`: This tells the browser to disable browser caching.
10. `Don't Sniff Mimetype`: This forces the browser to disable mime sniffing or guessing the content type of a served file.

11. `Referrer Policy`: The referrer headers provide the server with data regarding where the request was originated. It allows developers to disable it, or set a stricter policy for setting a `referrer` header.

12. `XSS Filter`: This prevents reflected cross-site scripting (XSS) attacks by setting the `X-XSS-Protection` header.

Getting ready

In this recipe, we will use most of the middleware functions provided by Helmet to secure our ExpressJS web application against common attacks. Before you start, create a new `package.json` file with the following content:

```
{
    "dependencies": {
        "body-parser": "1.18.2",
        "express": "4.16.3",
        "helmet": "3.12.0",
        "uuid": "3.2.1"
    }
}
```

Then, install the dependencies by opening a Terminal and running:

```
npm install
```

How to do it...

1. Create a new file named `secure-helmet.js`

2. Include the ExpressJS, helmet, and body NPM modules:

```
const express = require('express')
const helmet = require('helmet')
const bodyParser = require('body-parser')
const uuid = require('uuid/v1')
const app = express()
```

3. Generate a random ID which will be used for `nonce` which is an HTML attribute used for whitelist which scripts or styles are allowed to be executed inline in the HTML code:

```
const suid = uuid()
```

4. Use body parser to parse JSON request body for `json` and `application/csp-report` content types. `application/csp-report` is a content type that contains a JSON request body of type `json` which is sent by the browser when one or several CSP rules are violated:

```
app.use(bodyParser.json({
    type: ['json', 'application/csp-report'],
}))
```

5. Use the `Content Security Policy` middleware function to define directives. `defaultSrc` specifies where resources can be loaded from. The `self` option specifies to load resources only from your own domain. We will use `none` instead, which means that no resources will be loaded. However, because we are whitelisting `scriptSrc`, we will be able to load Javascript scripts but only the ones that have the `nonce` that we will specify. The `reportUri` is used to tell the browser where to send violation reports of our `Content Security Policy`:

```
app.use(helmet.contentSecurityPolicy({
    directives: {
        // By default do not allow unless whitelisted
        defaultSrc: [`'none'`],
         // Only allow scripts with this nonce
        scriptSrc: [`'nonce-${suid}'`],
        reportUri: '/csp-violation',
    }
}))
```

6. Add a route method to handle `POST` request for path "`/csp-violation`" to receive violation reports from the client:

```
app.post('/csp-violation', (request, response, next) => {
    const { body } = request
    if (body) {
        console.log('CSP Report Violation:')
        console.dir(body, { colors: true, depth: 5 })
    }
    response.status(204).send()
})
```

7. Use the `DNS Prefetch Control` middleware to disable prefetch of resources:

```
app.use(helmet.dnsPrefetchControl({ allow: false }))
```

8. Use the `Frameguard` middleware function to disable your application from being loaded inside a `iframe`:

```
app.use(helmet.frameguard({ action: 'deny' }))
```

9. Use the `hidePoweredBy` middleware function to replace the `X-Powered-By` header and set a fake one:

```
app.use(helmet.hidePoweredBy({
    setTo: 'Django/1.2.1 SVN-13336',
}))
```

10. Use the `ieNoOpen` middleware function to disable IE untrusted executions:

```
app.use(helmet.ieNoOpen())
```

11. Use the `noSniff` middleware function to disable mime-type guessing:

```
app.use(helmet.noSniff())
```

12. Use the `referrerPolicy` middleware function to make the header available only for our domain:

```
app.use(helmet.referrerPolicy({ policy: 'same-origin' }))
```

13. Use the `xssFilter` middleware function to prevent Reflected XSS attacks:

```
app.use(helmet.xssFilter())
```

14. Add a route method to handle GET requests on path "/" and serve a sample HTML content that will try to load an image from an external source, try to execute an inline script, and try to load an external script without a `nonce` specified. We will add a valid script as well that is allowed to be executed because a `nonce` attribute will be specified:

```
app.get('/', (request, response, next) => {
    response.send(`
    <!DOCTYPE html>
    <html lang="en">
    <head>
        <meta charset="utf-8">
        <title>Web App</title>
    </head>
     <body>
        <span id="txtlog"></span>
         <img alt="Evil Picture" src="http://evil.com/pic.jpg">
```

```
        <script>
            alert('This does not get executed!')
        </script>
        <script src="http://evil.com/evilstuff.js"></script>
        <script nonce="${suid}">
            document.getElementById('txtlog')
                .innerText = 'Hello World!'
        </script>
    </body>
  </html>
 `)
})
```

15. Listen on port 1337 for new connections:

```
app.listen(
    1337,
    () => console.log('Web Server running on port 1337'),
)
```

16. Save the file

17. Open a terminal and run:

```
node secure-helmet.js
```

18. To see the results, in your web browser, navigate to:

```
http://localhost:1337/
```

How it works...

How everything works is pretty straight forward with `Helmet`. You specify the security measures you want to implement by choosing and applying a specific `Helmet` middleware function and `Helmet` will do the work of setting the right headers that will be sent to the client.

In the client side (web browser), everything just works by its own. The web browser is in charge of interpreting the headers sent by the server and applying the security policies. This also means that old browsers cannot support or understand all these headers. Saying that, there are not many good reasons why you would want to support old web browsers if you have security in mind for your application.

If you are using Chrome, for instance, you should be able to see something similar to this in the console:

```
⊗ Failed to set referrer policy: The value 'same-origin'        localhost/:1
  is not one of 'no-referrer', 'no-referrer-when-downgrade', 'origin',
  'origin-when-cross-origin', or 'unsafe-url'. The referrer policy has
  been left unchanged.
⊗ Refused to load the image 'http://evil.com/pic.jpg'          localhost/:9
  because it violates the following Content Security Policy directive:
  "default-src 'none'". Note that 'img-src' was not explicitly set, so
  'default-src' is used as a fallback.
⊗ Refused to execute inline script because it violates the     localhost/:9
  following Content Security Policy directive: "script-src 'nonce-
  MC41NTY3NjI2ODI5NzQxNzUy'". Either the 'unsafe-inline' keyword, a hash
  ('sha256-rFKp17X6XMQNDA0G7t/e42CiZX1fKuJxRotykwjTsEc='), or a nonce
  ('nonce-...') is required to enable inline execution.
⊗ Refused to load the script                                    localhost/:1
  'http://evil.com/evilstuff.js' because it violates the following
  Content Security Policy directive: "script-src 'nonce-
  MC41NTY3NjI2ODI5NzQxNzUy'".
```

Chrome Dev Tools | Console displaying CSP violation

1. In the Terminal, you should be able to see similar output to the following that is sent by the browser:

```
CSP Report Violation: {
    "csp-report": {
        "document-uri": "http://localhost:1337/",
        "referrer": "",
        "violated-directive": "img-src",
        "effective-directive": "img-src",
        "original-policy": "default-src 'none'; script-src
'[nonce]'; report-uri /csp-violation",
        "disposition": "enforce",
        "blocked-uri": "http://evil.com/pic.jpg",
        "line-number": 9,
        "source-file": "http://localhost:1337/",
        "status-code": 200
    }
}
CSP Report Violation: {
    "csp-report": {
        "document-uri": "http://localhost:1337/",
        "referrer": "",
        "violated-directive": "script-src",
        "effective-directive": "script-src",
        "original-policy": "default-src 'none'; script-src
```

```
        '[nonce]'; report-uri /csp-violation",
              "disposition": "enforce",
              "blocked-uri": "inline",
              "line-number": 9,
              "status-code": 200
          }
      }
  CSP Report Violation: {
      "csp-report": {
          "document-uri": "http://localhost:1337/",
          "referrer": "",
          "violated-directive": "script-src",
          "effective-directive": "script-src",
          "original-policy": "default-src 'none'; script-src
  '[nonce]'; report-uri /csp-violation",
          "disposition": "enforce",
          "blocked-uri": "http://evil.com/evilstuff.js",
          "status-code": 200
      }
  }
```

Using template engines

Template engines allow you to generate HTML code in a more convenient way. Templates or views can be written in any format, interpreted by a template engine that will replace variables with other values, and finally transform to HTML.

A big list of template engines that work out of the box with ExpressJS, is available in the official website at `https://github.com/expressjs/express/wiki#template-engines`.

Getting ready

In this recipe, you will build your own template engine. To develop and use your own template engine, you will first need to register it, then define the path where the views are located, and finally tell ExpressJS which template engine to use.

```
app.engine('...', (path, options, callback) => { ... });
app.set('views', './');
app.set('view engine', '...');
```

Before you start, create a new `package.json` file with the following content:

```
{
    "dependencies": {
        "express": "4.16.3"
    }
}
```

Then, install the dependencies by opening a terminal and running:

```
npm install
```

How to do it...

First create a `views` directory which will contain a simple template:

1. Create a new directory named `views`
2. Create a new file named `home.tpl` inside our `views` directory
3. Add the following code:

```
<!DOCTYPE html>
 <html lang="en">
<head>
    <meta charset="utf-8">
    <title>Using Template Engines</title>
</head>
<body>
    <section role="application">
        <h1>%title%</h1>
        <p>%description%</p>
    </section>
</body>
</html>
```

4. Save the file

Now, create a new template engine that will transform the previous template into HTML and replace `%[var]%` with the options provided:

1. Move out of the `views` directory
2. Create a new file named `my-template-engine.js`

3. Include the ExpressJS and fs (file system) libraries. Then, initialize a new ExpressJS application:

```
const express = require('express')
const fs = require('fs')
const app = express()
```

4. Use the `engine` method to register a new template engine named `tpl`. We will read the file's content and replace `%[var]%` with the one specified in the `options` object:

```
app.engine('tpl', (filepath, options, callback) => {
    fs.readFile(filepath, (err, data) => {
        if (err) {
            return callback(err)
        }
        const content = data
            .toString()
            .replace(/%[a-z]+%/gi, (match) => {
                const variable = match.replace(/%/g, '')
                if (Reflect.has(options, variable)) {
                    return options[variable]
                }
                return match
            })
        return callback(null, content)
    })
})
```

5. Define the path where the views are located. Our template is located in the `views` directory:

```
app.set('views', './views')
```

6. Tell ExpressJS to use our template engine:

```
app.set('view engine', 'tpl')
```

7. Add a route method to handle GET requests for path "/" and render our home template. Provide the title and description options which will replace %title% and %description% in our template:

```
app.get('/', (request, response, next) => {
    response.render('home', {
        title: 'Hello',
         description: 'World!',
    })
})
```

8. Listen on port 1337 for new connections:

```
app.listen(
    1337,
    () => console.log('Web Server running on port 1337'),
)
```

9. Save the file

10. Open a terminal and run:

```
node my-template-engine.js
```

11. In your browser, navigate to:

```
http://localhost:1337/
```

 The template engine we just have wrote doesn't escape HTML characters. That means, you should be careful if replacing those properties with data gotten from the client because it may be vulnerable to XSS attacks. You may want to use a template engine from the official ExpressJS website that is safer.

Debugging your ExpressJS web application

Debugging information on ExpressJS about all of the cycle of a web application is something simple. ExpressJS uses the **debug** NPM module internally to log information. Unlike console.log, **debug** logs can easily be disabled on production mode.

Getting ready

In this recipe, you will see how to debug your ExpressJS web application. Before you start, create a new `package.json` file with the following content:

```
{
    "dependencies": {
        "debug": "3.1.0",
        "express": "4.16.3"
    }
}
```

Then, install the dependencies by opening a terminal and running:

```
npm install
```

How to do it...

1. Create a new file named `debugging.js`
2. Initialize a new ExpressJS application:

```
const express = require('express')
const app = express()
```

3. Add a route method to handle GET requests for any path:

```
app.get('*', (request, response, next) => {
    response.send('Hello there!')
})
```

4. Listen on port `1337` for new connections:

```
app.listen(
    1337,
    () => console.log('Web Server running on port 1337'),
)
```

5. Save the file
6. Open a terminal and run:
7. On Windows:

```
set DEBUG=express:* node debugging.js
```

8. On Linux or MacOS:

```
DEBUG=express:* node debugging.js
```

9. In your web browser, navigate to:

```
http://localhost:1337/
```

10. Observe your terminal's output for logs

How it works...

The DEBUG environment variable is used to tell the **debug** module which parts of the ExpressJS application to debug. In our previously written code, express:* tells the debug module to log everything related to the express application.

We could use DEBUG=express:router to displays logs related to the Router or routing of ExpressJS.

There's more...

You can use the debug NPM module in your own projects. For example:

1. Create a new file named myapp.js
2. Add the following code:

```
const express = require('express')
const app = express()
const debug = require('debug')('myapp')
app.get('*', (request, response, next) => {
    debug('Request:', request.originalUrl)
    response.send('Hello there!')
})
app.listen(
    1337,
    () => console.log('Web Server running on port 1337'),
)
```

3. Save the file
4. Open a terminal and run:
5. On Windows:

```
set DEBUG=myapp node myapp.js
```

6. On Linux and MacOS:

```
DEBUG=myapp node myapp.js
```

7. In your web browser, navigate to:
8. Observe your Terminal's output. It would display something like:

```
Web Server running on port 1337
  myapp Request: / +0ms
```

You can use the DEBUG environment variable to tell the debug module to displays logs not only for myapp but also for ExpressJS like so:

On Windows:

```
set DEBUG=myapp,express:* node myapp.js
```

On Linux and MacOS:

```
DEBUG=myapp,express:* node myapp.js
```

3
Building a RESTful API

In this chapter, we will cover the following recipes:

- CRUD operations using ExpressJS' route methods
- CRUD operations with Mongoose
- Using Mongoose query builders
- Defining document instance methods
- Defining static model methods
- Writing middleware functions for Mongoose
- Writing custom validators for Mongoose's schemas
- Building a RESTful API to manage users with ExpressJS and Mongoose

Technical requirements

You will be required to have an IDE, Visual Studio Code, Node.js and MongoDB. You will also need to install Git, in order use the Git repository of this book.

The code files of this chapter can be found on GitHub:
https://github.com/PacktPublishing/MERN-Quick-Start-Guide/tree/master/Chapter03

Check out the following video to see the code in action:
https://goo.gl/73dE6u

duction

Representation State Transfer (REST) is an architectural style that the web was built on. More specifically, the HTTP 1.1 protocol standards were built using the REST principles. REST provides a representation of a resource. **URLs (Uniform Resource Locator)** are used to define the location of a resource and tell the browser where it is located.

A RESTful API is a web service API that adheres to this architectural style.

The most commonly used HTTP verbs or methods are: POST, GET, PUT, and DELETE. These methods are the basis for persistent storage and are known as **CRUD** operations **(Create, Read, Update, and Delete)**.

In this chapter, the recipes will be focused on building a RESTful API using the REST architectural style with ExpressJS and Mongoose.

CRUD operations using ExpressJS' route methods

ExpressJS' router has equivalent methods to handle HTTP methods. In other words, the HTTP methods POST, GET, PUT, and DELETE can be handled by this code:

```
/* Add a new user */
app.post('/users', (request, response, next) => { })
/* Get user */
app.get('/users/:id', (request, response, next) => { })
/* Update a user */
app.put('/users/:id', (request, response, next) => { })
/* Delete a user */
app.delete('/users/:id', (request, response, next) => { })
```

It's good to think of every URL as a noun and because of that a verb can act on it. In fact, HTTP methods are also known as HTTP verbs. If we think about them as verbs, when a request is made to our RESTful API, they can be understood as:

- Post a user
- Get a user
- Update a user
- Delete a user.

In the **MVC (model-view-controller)** architectural pattern, controllers are in charge of transforming input to something a model or view can understand. In other words, they transform input into actions or commands and sends them to the model or view to update accordingly.

ExpressJS' route methods usually act as controllers. They just get input from a client such as a request from the browser, and then converts the input to actions. These actions are then sent to the model, which is the business logic of your application, such as a mongoose model, or to a view (a ReactJS client application) to update.

Getting ready

Keeping in mind that we can invoke an action over a resource using HTTP methods, we will see how to build a RESTful API web service based on those concepts. Before you start, create a new `package.json` file with the following code:

```
{
  "dependencies": {
    "express": "4.16.3",
    "node-fetch": "2.1.1",
    "uuid": "3.2.1"
  }
}
```

Then, install the dependencies by opening a terminal and running this line of code:

```
npm install
```

How to do it...

Build a RESTful API with an in-memory database or an array of objects that will contain a list of users. We will allow CRUD operations using HTTP methods to add a new user, get a user or list of users, update a user's data, and delete a user:

1. Create a new file named `restfulapi.js`

2. Import the packages that we need and create an ExpressJS application:

```
const express = require('express')
const uuid = require('uuid')
const app = express()
```

3. Define an in-memory database:

```
let data = [
    { id: uuid(), name: 'Bob' },
    { id: uuid(), name: 'Alice' },
]
```

4. Create a model which will contain functions for making CRUD operations:

```
const usr = {
    create(name) {
        const user = { id: uuid(), name }
        data.push(user)
        return user
    },
    read(id) {
        if (id === 'all') return data
        return data.find(user => user.id === id)
    },
    update(id, name) {
        const user = data.find(usr => usr.id === id)
        if (!user) return { status: 'User not found' }
        user.name = name
        return user
    },
    delete(id) {
        data = data.filter(user => user.id !== id)
        return { status: 'deleted', id }
    }
}
```

5. Add a request handler for the `post` method that will be used as a `Create` operation. A new user will be added to the `data` array:

```
app.post('/users/:name', (req, res) => {
    res.status(201).json(usr.create(req.params.name))
})
```

6. Add a request handler for the `get` method that will be used as a `Read` or `Retrieve` operation. If an `id` is given, look for the user in the `data` array. However, If the given `id` is `"all"`, it will return the whole list of users:

```
app.get('/users/:id', (req, res) => {
    res.status(200).json(usr.read(req.params.id))
})
```

7. Add a request handler for the `put` method that will be used as an `Update` operation. An `id` needs to be provided in order to update a specific user in the `data` array:

```
app.put('/users/:id=:name', (req, res) => {
    res.status(200).json(usr.update(
        req.params.id,
        req.params.name,
    ))
})
```

8. Add a request handler for the `delete` method that will be used as a `Delete` operation. It will look for the user in the `data` array and remove it:

```
app.delete('/users/:id', (req, res) => {
    res.status(200).json(usr.delete(req.params.id))
})
```

9. Start your application listening on port `1337` for new connections:

```
app.listen(
    1337,
    () => console.log('Web Server running on port 1337'),
)
```

10. Save the file.
11. Open a Terminal and run this code:

```
node restfulapi.js
```

Let's test it...

To make it simple, create a script that will request and make CRUD operations on our RESTful API server:

1. Create a new file named `test-restfulapi.js`.
2. Add the following code:

```
const fetch = require('node-fetch')
const r = async (url, method) => (
    await fetch(`http://localhost:1337${url}`, { method })
        .then(r => r.json())
)
const log = (...obj) => (
    obj.forEach(o => console.dir(o, { colors: true }))
)
async function test() {
    const users = await r('/users/all', 'get')
    const { id } = users[0]
    const getById = await r(`/users/${id}`, 'get')
    const updateById = await r(`/users/${id}=John`, 'put')
    const deleteById = await r(`/users/${id}`, 'delete')
    const addUsr = await r(`/users/Smith`, 'post')
    const getAll = await r('/users/all', 'get')
    log('[GET] users:', users)
    log(`[GET] a user with id="${id}":`, getById)
    log(`[PUT] a user with id="${id}":`, updateById)
    log(`[POST] a new user:`, addUsr)
    log(`[DELETE] a user with id="${id}":`, deleteById)
    log(`[GET] users:`, getAll)
}
test()
```

3. Save the file.
4. Open a new Terminal and run this code:

```
node test-restfulapi.js
```

How it works...

Our RESTful API application will be running locally on port `1337`. When running the test code, it will connect to it and make several requests using different HTTP methods to create a user, retrieve a user, update a user, and delete a user. All the operations will be logged in the Terminal.

If you prefer to test it yourself, you can replace all the code inside the `test` function, and use the `r` function to make custom requests. For instance, to create a new user called `Smith`:

```
r(`/users/Smith`, 'post')
```

CRUD operations with Mongoose

One of many reasons why developers opt to use Mongoose instead of the official MongoDB driver for Node.js is that it allows you to create data structures with ease by using schemas and also because of the built-in validation. MongoDB is a document-oriented database, meaning that the structure of the documents varies.

In the MVC architectural pattern, Mongoose is often used for creating models that shape or define data structures.

This is how a typical Mongoose schema would be defined and then compiled into a model:

```
const PersonSchema = new Schema({
    firstName: String,
    lastName: String,
})
const Person = connection.model('Person', PersonSchema)
```

Model names should be in singular since Mongoose will make them plural and lowercase them when saving the collection to the database. For instance, if the model is named "User", it will be saved as a collection named "users" in MongoDB. Mongoose includes an internal dictionary to pluralize common names. That means if your model's name is a common name, such as "Person", it will be saved in MongoDB as a collection named "people".

Mongoose allows the following types to define a schema's path or document structure:

- String
- Number
- Boolean
- Array
- Date
- Buffer
- Mixed
- Objectid
- Decimal128

A schema type can be declared by using directly the global constructor function for String, Number, Boolean, Buffer, and Date:

```
const { Schema} = require('mongoose')
const PersonSchema = new Schema({
    name: String,
    age: Number,
    isSingle: Boolean,
    birthday: Date,
    description: Buffer,
})
```

These schema types are also available under an object called SchemaTypes in the exported mongoose object:

```
const { Schema, SchemaTypes } = require('mongoose')
const PersonSchema = new Schema({
    name: SchemaTypes.String,
    age: SchemaTypes.Number,
    isSingle: SchemaTypes.Boolean,
    birthday: SchemaTypes.Date,
    description: SchemaTypes.Buffer,
})
```

Schema types can be declared using an object as a property that gives you more control over the specific schema type. Take the following code, for example:

```
const { Schema } = require('mongoose')
const PersonSchema = new Schema({
    name: { type: String, required: true, default: 'Unknown' },
    age: { type: Number, min: 18, max: 80, required: true },
    isSingle: { type: Boolean },
    birthday: { type: Date, required: true },
    description: { type: Buffer },
})
```

Schema types can also be arrays. For instance, if we want a field to define what are the things the user likes in an array of strings, you could use this code:

```
const PersonSchema = new Schema({
    name: String,
    age: Number,
    likes: [String],
})
```

To learn more about schema types, visit the official Mongoose documentation website: `http://mongoosejs.com/docs/schematypes.html`.

Getting ready

In this recipe, you will see how to define a schema and perform CRUD operation on the database collection. First, ensure that you have MongoDB installed and it's running. As an alternative, if you prefer, a MongoDB **DBaaS (Database as a Service)** instance in the cloud will also do. Before you start, create a new `package.json` file with the following code:

```
{
  "dependencies": {
    "mongoose": "5.0.11"
  }
}
```

Then, install the dependencies by opening a Terminal and running this code:

```
npm install
```

How to do it...

Define a user schema that will contain user's first name, last name, and an array of strings that define the things the user likes:

1. Create a new file named `mongoose-models.js`

2. Include the Mongoose NPM module. Then, create a connection to MongoDB:

```
const mongoose = require('mongoose')
const { connection, Schema } = mongoose
mongoose.connect(
    'mongodb://localhost:27017/test'
).catch(console.error)
```

3. Define a schema:

```
const UserSchema = new Schema({
    firstName: String,
    lastName: String,
    likes: [String],
})
```

4. Compile the schema into a model:

```
const User = mongoose.model('User', UserSchema)
```

5. Define a function that will be used for adding new users:

```
const addUser = (firstName, lastName) => new User({
    firstName,
    lastName,
}).save()
```

6. Define a function that will be used for retrieving a user from the collection of users by its `id`:

```
const getUser = (id) => User.findById(id)
```

7. Define a function that will remove the user from the collection of users by its `id`:

```
const removeUser = (id) => User.remove({ id })
```

8. Define an event listener that will perform CRUD operations once the there is a connection to the database. First, add a new user and save it. Then, retrieve the same user using its `id`. Next, modify the user's properties and save it. Finally, remove the user from the collection by its `id`:

```
connection.once('connected', async () => {
    try {
        // Create
        const newUser = await addUser('John', 'Smith')
        // Read
        const user = await getUser(newUser.id)
        // Update
        user.firstName = 'Jonny'
        user.lastName = 'Smithy'
        user.likes = [
            'cooking',
            'watching movies',
            'ice cream',
        ]
        await user.save()
        console.log(JSON.stringify(user, null, 4))
        // Delete
        await removeUser(user.id)
    } catch (error) {
        console.dir(error.message, { colors: true })
    } finally {
        await connection.close()
    }
})
```

9. Save the file.
10. Open a Terminal and run this code:

```
node mongoose-models.js
```

Executing the previous command in the Terminal, if successful, would display something similar to the following, for instance, a code such as this:

```
{
    "likes": [
    "cooking",
        "watching movies",
        "ice cream"
        ],
    "_id": "[some id]",
    "firstName": "Jonny",
    "lastName": "Smithy",
```

```
        "__v": 1
    }
```

See also

- Chapter 1, *Introduction to the MERN Stack*, section *Installing NPM Packages*
- Chapter 1, *Introduction to the MERN Stack*, section *Installing MongoDB*

Using Mongoose query builders

Every Mongoose model has static helper methods to do several kinds of operations, such as retrieving a document. When a callback is passed to these helper methods, the operation is executed immediately:

```
const user = await User.findOne({
    firstName: 'Jonh',
    age: { $lte: 30 },
}, (error, document) => {
    if (error) return console.log(error)
    console.log(document)
})
```

Otherwise, if there is no defined callback, a *query builder interface* is returned, which can be later executed:

```
const user = User.findOne({
    firstName: 'Jonh',
    age: { $lte: 30 },
})
user.exec((error, document) => {
    if (error) return console.log(error)
    console.log(document)
})
```

Queries also have a .then function which can be used as a Promise. When .then is called, it first executes the query internally with .exec which then returns a Promise. This allows us to use async/await as well. Inside a async function, for instance:

```
try {
    const user = await User.findOne({
        firstName: 'Jonh',
        age: { $lte: 30 },
```

```
    })
    console.log(user)
} catch (error) {
    console.log(error)
}
```

There are two ways that we can make a query. One is by providing a JSON object that is used as a condition and the other way allows you to create a query using chaining syntax. The chaining syntax will feel more comfortable to developers who are more familiar with SQL databases. For example:

```
try {
    const user = await User.findOne()
  .where('firstName', 'John')
        .where('age').lte(30)
    console.log(user)
}       catch (error) {
    console.log(error)
}
```

Getting ready

In this recipe, you will build up queries using chaining syntax and using `async/await` functions. First, ensure that you have MongoDB installed and it's running. As an alternative, if you prefer, a MongoDB DBaaS instance in the cloud will also do. Before you start, create a new `package.json` file with the following code:

```
{
  "dependencies": {
    "mongoose": "5.0.11"
  }
}
```

Then, install the dependencies by opening a Terminal and running:

npm install

How to do it...

1. Create a new file named `chaining-queries.js`

2. Include the Mongoose NPM module. Then, create a new connection:

```
const mongoose = require('mongoose')
const { connection, Schema } = mongoose
mongoose.connect(
    'mongodb://localhost:27017/test'
).catch(console.error)
```

3. Define a schema:

```
const UserSchema = new Schema({
    firstName: String,
    lastName: String,
    age: Number,
})
```

4. Compile the schema into a model:

```
const User = mongoose.model('User', UserSchema)
```

5. Once connected to the database, add a new document to the collection of users. Then, using chaining syntax, query for the recently created user. Additionally, use the `select` method to restrict which fields are retrieved from the document:

```
connection.once('connected', async () => {
    try {
        const user = await new User({
            firstName: 'John',
            lastName: 'Snow',
            age: 30,
        }).save()
        const findUser = await User.findOne()
            .where('firstName').equals('John')
            .where('age').lte(30)
            .select('lastName age')
        console.log(JSON.stringify(findUser, null, 4))
        await user.remove()
    } catch (error) {
        console.dir(error.message, { colors: true })
    } finally {
        await connection.close()
    }
})
```

6. Save the file
7. Open a Terminal and run:

```
node chaining-queries.js
```

See also

- `Chapter 1`, *Introduction to the MERN Stack*, section *Installing NPM Packages*
- `Chapter 1`, *Introduction to the MERN Stack*, section *Installing MongoDB*

Defining document instance methods

Documents have their own built-in instance methods such as `save` and `remove`. However, we can write our own instance methods as well.

Documents are instances of models. They can be explicitly created:

```
const instance = new Model()
```

Or they can be the result of a query:

```
Model.findOne([conditions]).then((instance) => {})
```

Document instance methods are defined in the schema. All schemas have a method called `method` which allows you to define custom instance methods.

Getting ready

In this recipe, you will define a schema and custom document instance methods for modifying and reading document properties. First, ensure that you have MongoDB installed and it's running. As an alternative, if you prefer, a MongoDB DBaaS instance in the cloud will also do. Before you start, create a new `package.json` file with the following code:

```
{
  "dependencies": {
    "mongoose": "5.0.11"
  }
}
```

Then, install the dependencies by opening a Terminal and running this code:

```
npm install
```

How to do it...

1. Create a new file named `document-methods.js`
2. Include the Mongoose NPM module. Then, create a new connection to MongoDB:

```
const mongooconst mongoose = require('mongoose')
const { connection, Schema } = mongoose
mongoose.connect(
    'mongodb://localhost:27017/test'
).catch(console.error)
```

3. Define a schema:

```
const UserSchema = new Schema({
    firstName: String,
    lastName: String,
    likes: [String],
})
```

4. Define a document instance method for setting a user's first name and last name from a string containing their full name:

```
UserSchema.method('setFullName', function setFullName(v) {
    const fullName = String(v).split(' ')
    this.lastName = fullName[0] || ''
    this.firstName = fullName[1] || ''
})
```

5. Define a document instance method for getting a user's full name concatenating the `firstName` and `lastName` properties:

```
UserSchema.method('getFullName', function getFullName() {
    return `${this.lastName} ${this.firstName}`
})
```

6. Define a document instance method named `loves` that will expect one argument that will add to the `likes` array of strings:

```
UserSchema.method('loves', function loves(stuff) {
    this.likes.push(stuff)
})
```

7. Define a document instance method named `dislikes` which will remove one thing previous liked by the user from the `likes` array:

```
UserSchema.method('dislikes', function dislikes(stuff) {
    this.likes = this.likes.filter(str => str !== stuff)
})
```

8. Compile the schema into a model:

```
const User = mongoose.model('User', UserSchema)
```

9. Once Mongoose is connected to the database, create a new user and use `setFullName` method to populate the fields `firstName` and `lastName`, then use the `loves` method to populate the `likes` array. Next, use chaining syntax to query for the user in the collection and use the `dislikes` method to remove `"snakes"` from the `likes` array:

```
connection.once('connected', async () => {
    try {
        // Create
        const user = new User()
        user.setFullName('Huang Jingxuan')
        user.loves('kitties')
        user.loves('strawberries')
        user.loves('snakes')
        await user.save()
        // Update
        const person = await User.findOne()
            .where('firstName', 'Jingxuan')
            .where('likes').in(['snakes', 'kitties'])
        person.dislikes('snakes')
        await person.save()
        // Display
        console.log(person.getFullName())
        console.log(JSON.stringify(person, null, 4))
        // Remove
        await user.remove()
    } catch (error) {
        console.dir(error.message, { colors: true })
```

```
        } finally {
            await connection.close()
        }
    })
```

10. Save the file.
11. Open a Terminal and run this code:

```
node document-methods.js
```

There's more...

Document instance methods can also be defined using the `methods`, schema property. For instance:

```
UserSchema.methods.setFullName = function setFullName(v) {
    const fullName = String(v).split(' ')
    this.lastName = fullName[0] || ''
    this.firstName = fullName[1] || ''
}
```

See also

- `Chapter 1`, *Introduction to the MERN Stack*, section *Installing NPM Packages*
- `Chapter 1`, *Introduction to the MERN Stack*, section *Installing MongoDB*

Defining static model methods

Models have built-in static methods such as `find`, `findOne`, and `findOneAndRemove`. Mongoose allow us to define custom static model methods as well. Static model methods are defined in the schema in the same way as document instance methods are.

Schemas have a property called `statics` which is an object. All the methods defined inside the `statics` object are passed to the model. Static model methods can also be defined by calling the `static` schema method.

Getting ready

In this recipe, you will define a schema and custom static model method for expanding your model's capabilities. First, ensure that you have MongoDB installed and it's running. As an alternative, if you prefer, a MongoDB DBaaS instance in the cloud will also do. Before you start, create a new `package.json` file with the following code:

```
{
  "dependencies": {
    "mongoose": "5.0.11"
  }
}
```

Then, install the dependencies by opening a Terminal and running:

```
npm install
```

How to do it...

Define a static model method called `getByFullName` that will allow you to search for a specific user using their full name:

1. Create a new file named `static-methods.js`
2. Include the Mongoose NPM module and create a new connection to your MongoDB:

```
const mongoose = require('mongoose')
const { connection, Schema } = mongoose
mongoose.connect(
    'mongodb://localhost:27017/test'
).catch(console.error)
```

3. Define a schema:

```
const UsrSchm = new Schema({
    firstName: String,
    lastName: String,
    likes: [String],
})
```

4. Define `getByFullName` static model method:

```
UsrSchm.static('getByFullName', function getByFullName(v) {
    const fullName = String(v).split(' ')
    const lastName = fullName[0] || ''
    const firstName = fullName[1] || ''
    return this.findOne()
        .where('firstName').equals(firstName)
        .where('lastName').equals(lastName)
})
```

5. Compile the schema into a model:

```
const User = mongoose.model('User', UsrSchm)
```

6. Once connected, create a new user and save it. Then, use the `getByFullName` static model method to look for the user in the collection of users using their full name:

```
connection.once('connected', async () => {
    try {
        // Create
        const user = new User({
            firstName: 'Jingxuan',
            lastName: 'Huang',
            likes: ['kitties', 'strawberries'],
        })
        await user.save()
        // Read
        const person = await User.getByFullName(
            'Huang Jingxuan'
        )
        console.log(JSON.stringify(person, null, 4))
        await person.remove()
        await connection.close()
    } catch (error) {
        console.log(error.message)
    }
})
```

6. Save the file
7. Open a Terminal and run this code:

```
node static-methods.js
```

There's more...

Static model methods can also be defined using the `statics` schema property. For instance:

```
UsrSchm.statics.getByFullName = function getByFullName(v) {
    const fullName = String(v).split(' ')
    const lastName = fullName[0] || ''
    const firstName = fullName[1] || ''
    return this.findOne()
        .where('firstName').equals(firstName)
        .where('lastName').equals(lastName)
}
```

See also

- Chapter 1, *Introduction to the MERN Stack*, section *Installing NPM Packages*
- Chapter 1, *Introduction to the MERN Stack*, section *Installing MongoDB*

Writing middleware functions for Mongoose

Middleware functions in Mongoose are also called `hooks`. There are two types of hooks `pre hooks` and `post hooks`.

The difference, between `pre hooks` and post hooks, is pretty simple. `pre hooks` are called before a method is called, and `post hooks` are called after. For example:

```
const UserSchema = new Schema({
    firstName: String,
    lastName: String,
    fullName: String,
})
UserSchema.pre('save', async function preSave() {
    this.fullName = `${this.lastName} ${this.firstName}`
})
UserSchema.post('save', async function postSave(doc) {
    console.log(`New user created: ${doc.fullName}`)
})
const User = mongoose.model('User', UserSchema)
```

And later on, once the connection is made to the database, within an `async` function:

```
const user = new User({
    firstName: 'John',
    lastName: 'Smith',
})
await user.save()
```

Once the `save` method is called, the `pre hook` is executed first. After the document is saved, the `post hook` is then executed. In the previous example, it will display in the Terminal output the following text:

New user created: Smith John

There are four different types of middleware functions in Mongoose: document middleware, model middleware, aggregate middleware, and query middleware. All of them are defined on the schema level. The difference is, when the hooks are executed, the context of`this` refers to the document, model, the aggregation object, or the query object.

 All types of middleware support pre and post hooks

Getting ready

In this recipe, we will see how three of these types of middleware functions work in Mongoose:

- Document middleware
- Model middleware
- Query middleware

First, ensure that you have MongoDB installed and it's running. As an alternative, if you prefer, a MongoDB DBaaS instance in the cloud will also do. Before you start, create a new `package.json` file with the following code:

```
{
  "dependencies": {
    "mongoose": "5.0.11"
  }
}
```

Then, install the dependencies by opening a Terminal and running:

```
npm install
```

How to do it...

In document middleware functions, the context of `this` refers to the document. A document has the following built-in methods and you can define `hooks` for them:

- `init`: This is called internally, immediately after a document is returned from MongoDB. Mongoose uses setters for marking the document as modified or which fields of the document were modified. `init` initializes the document without setters.
- `validate`: This executes built-in and custom set validation rules for the document.
- `save`: This saves the document in the database.
- `remove`: This removes the document from the database.

Document middleware functions

Create `pre` and `post` hooks for the document built-in methods:

1. Create a new file named `1-document-middleware.js`
2. Include the Mongoose NPM module and create a new connection to your MongoDB:

```
const mongoose = require('mongoose')
const { connection, Schema } = mongoose
mongoose.connect(
    'mongodb://localhost:27017/test'
).catch(console.error)
```

3. Define a schema:

```
const UserSchema = new Schema({
    firstName: { type: String, required: true },
    lastName: { type: String, required: true },
})
```

4. Add a pre and post hook for the `init` document method:

```
UserSchema.pre('init', async function preInit() {
    console.log('A document is going to be initialized.')
})
UserSchema.post('init', async function postInit() {
    console.log('A document was initialized.')
})
```

5. Add a pre and post hook for the `validate` document method:

```
UserSchema.pre('validate', async function preValidate() {
    console.log('A document is going to be validated.')
})
UserSchema.post('validate', async function postValidate() {
    console.log('All validation rules were executed.')
})
```

6. Add a pre and post hook for the `save` document method:

```
UserSchema.pre('save', async function preSave() {
    console.log('Preparing to save the document')
})
UserSchema.post('save', async function postSave() {
    console.log(`A doc was saved id=${this.id}`)
})
```

7. Add a pre and post hook for the `remove` document method:

```
UserSchema.pre('remove', async function preRemove() {
    console.log(`Doc with id=${this.id} will be removed`)
})
UserSchema.post('remove', async function postRemove() {
    console.log(`Doc with id=${this.id} was removed`)
})
```

8. Compile the schema into a model:

```
const User = mongoose.model('User', UserSchema)
```

9. Once a new connection is established, create a document and perform some basic operations such as saving, retrieving, and deleting the document:

```
connection.once('connected', async () => {
    try {
        const user = new User({
            firstName: 'John',
            lastName: 'Smith',
        })
        await user.save()
        await User.findById(user.id)
        await user.remove()
        await connection.close()
    } catch (error) {
        await connection.close()
        console.dir(error.message, { colors: true })
    }
})
```

10. Save the file
11. Open a Terminal and run:

    node document-middleware.js

12. On the terminal, the output should display:

```
A document is going to be validated.
All validation rules were executed.
Preparing to save the document
A doc was saved id=[ID]
A document is going to be initialized.
A document was initialized.
Doc with id=[ID] will be removed
Doc with id=[ID] was removed
```

When you save a document, it first triggers the `validation` hooks that ensure that the fields pass the rules set by built-in validation rules or custom rules. In your code, the fields are marked as required. Then it will trigger the `save` hooks. After, using a model method to retrieve the recently created user from the database, once the document is retrieved, it triggers the `init` hooks. Finally, removing the document from the database triggers the `remove` hooks.

Within the hooks, you can interact with the document. For instance, the following `save` pre hook will modify the fields `firstName` and `lastName` to make them upper-cased strings:

```
UserSchema.pre('save', async function preSave() {
    this.firstName = this.firstName.toUpperCase()
    this.lastName = this.lastName.toUpperCase()
})
```

The same way, we can throw an error within the hook to prevent the next ones from being executed. For instance:

```
UserSchema.pre('save', async function preSave() {
    throw new Error('Doc was prevented from being saved.')
})
```

Query middleware functions are defined exactly as document middleware functions are. However, the context of `this` doesn't not refer to the document but instead to the query object. Query middleware functions are only supported in the following model and query functions:

- `count`: Counts the number of document that match a specific query condition
- `find`: Returns an array of documents that match a specific query condition
- `findOne`: Return a document that matches a specific query condition
- `findOneAndRemove`: Similar to `findOne`. However, after a document is found, it is removed
- `findOneAndUpdate`: Similar to `findOne` but once a document matching a specific query condition is found, the document can also be updated
- `update`: Update one or more documents that match a certain query condition

Query middleware functions

Create pre and post hooks for query built-in methods:

1. Create a new file named `2-query-middleware.js`
2. Include the Mongoose NPM module and create a new connection to your MongoDB:

```
const mongoose = require('mongoose')
const { connection, Schema } = mongoose
mongoose.connect(
    'mongodb://localhost:27017/test'
).catch(console.error)
```

3. Define a schema:

```
const UserSchema = new Schema({
    firstName: { type: String, required: true },
    lastName: { type: String, required: true },
})
```

4. Define pre and post hooks for the `count`, `find`, `findOne`, and `update` methods:

```
UserSchema.pre('count', async function preCount() {
    console.log(
        `Preparing to count document with this criteria:
        ${JSON.stringify(this._conditions)}`
    )
})
UserSchema.post('count', async function postCount(count) {
    console.log(`Counted ${count} documents that coincide`)
})
UserSchema.pre('find', async function preFind() {
    console.log(
        `Preparing to find all documents with criteria:
        ${JSON.stringify(this._conditions)}`
    )
})
UserSchema.post('find', async function postFind(docs) {
    console.log(`Found ${docs.length} documents`)
})
UserSchema.pre('findOne', async function prefOne() {
    console.log(
        `Preparing to find one document with criteria:
        ${JSON.stringify(this._conditions)}`
    )
})
UserSchema.post('findOne', async function postfOne(doc) {
    console.log(`Found 1 document:`, JSON.stringify(doc))
})
UserSchema.pre('update', async function preUpdate() {
    console.log(
        `Preparing to update all documents with criteria:
        ${JSON.stringify(this._conditions)}`
    )
})
UserSchema.post('update', async function postUpdate(r) {
    console.log(`${r.result.ok} document(s) were updated`)
})
```

5. Compile the schema into a model:

```
const User = mongoose.model('User', UserSchema)
```

6. Once the connection to the database is successfully made, create a document, save it, and use the methods for which we defined hooks for:

```
connection.once('connected', async () => {
    try {
        const user = new User({
            firstName: 'John',
            lastName: 'Smith',
        })
        await user.save()
        await User
            .where('firstName').equals('John')
            .update({ lastName: 'Anderson' })
        await User
            .findOne()
            .select(['lastName'])
            .where('firstName').equals('John')
        await User
            .find()
            .where('firstName').equals('John')
        await User
            .where('firstName').equals('Neo')
            .count()
        await user.remove()
    } catch (error) {
        console.dir(error, { colors: true })
    } finally {
        await connection.close()
    }
})
```

7. Save the file

8. Open a Terminal and run:

node query-middleware.js

9. On the terminal, the output should display something similar to:

```
Preparing to update all documents with criteria:
        {"firstName":"John"}
1 document(s) were updated
Preparing to find one document with criteria:
        {"firstName":"John"}
```

```
Found 1 document: {"_id":"[ID]","lastName":"Anderson"}
Preparing to find all documents with criteria:
        {"firstName":"John"}
Found 1 documents
Preparing to count document with this criteria:
        {"firstName":"Neo"}
Counted 0 documents that coincide
```

Finally, there is only one model instance method that supports hooks:

- `insertMany`: This validates an array of documents and saves them in the database only if all the documents in the array passed validation

As you probably guessed, a model middleware function is also defined in the same way as query middleware methods and document middleware methods are.

Model middleware functions

Create a `pre` and `post` hook for the `insertMany` model instance method:

1. Create a new file named `3-model-middleware.js`
2. Include the Mongoose NPM module and create a new connection to your MongoDB:

```
const mongoose = require('mongoose')
const { connection, Schema } = mongoose
mongoose.connect(
    'mongodb://localhost:27017/test'
).catch(console.error)
```

3. Define a schema:

```
const UserSchema = new Schema({
    firstName: { type: String, required: true },
    lastName: { type: String, required: true },
})
```

4. Define `pre` and `post` hooks for the `insertMany` model method:

```
UserSchema.pre('insertMany', async function prMany() {
    console.log('Preparing docs...')
})
UserSchema.post('insertMany', async function psMany(docs) {
    console.log('The following docs were created:n', docs)
})
```

5. Compile the schema into a model:

```
const User = mongoose.model('User', UserSchema)
```

6. Once a connection to the database was established, use the `insertMany` method to insert two documents at once:

```
connection.once('connected', async () => {
    try {
        await User.insertMany([
            { firstName: 'Leo', lastName: 'Smith' },
            { firstName: 'Neo', lastName: 'Jackson' },
        ])
    } catch (error) {
        console.dir(error, { colors: true })
    } finally {
        await connection.close()
    }
})
```

7. Save the file

8. Open a Terminal and run:

node query-middleware.js

9. On the Terminal, the output should display:

```
Preparing docs...
The following documents were created:
[ { firstName: 'Leo', lastName: 'Smith', _id: [id] },
  { firstName: 'Neo', lastName: 'Jackson', _id: [id] } ]
```

There's more...

It's useful to mark the fields as required to avoid having "null" values being saved in the database. An alternative is to set default values for the fields that are not explicitly defined in the creation time of the document. For instance:

```
const UserSchema = new Schema({
    name: {
        type: string,
        required: true,
        default: 'unknown',
    }
})
```

When a new document is created, if no path or property `name` is assigned, then it will assign the default value defined in the schema type option `default`.

 The schema type `default` option can also be a function. The value returned by calling this function is assigned as the default value.

Sub-documents or arrays can also be created by just adding brackets when defining the schema type. For instance:

```
const WishBoxSchema = new Schema({
    wishes: {
        type: [String],
        required: true,
        default: [
            'To be a snowman',
            'To be a string',
            'To be an example',
        ],
    },
})
```

When a new document is created, it will expect an array of strings in the `wishes` property or path. If no array is provided, then the default values will be used to create the document.

See also

- Chapter 1, *Introduction to the MERN Stack*, section *Installing NPM Packages*
- Chapter 1, *Introduction to the MERN Stack*, section *Installing MongoDB*

Writing custom validators for Mongoose's schemas

Mongoose has several built-in validation rules. For instance, if you define a property with a schema type of `string` and set it as `required`, two validation rules will be executed, one that checks for the property to be a valid `string` and another one for checking that the property is not `null` or `undefined`.

Custom validation rules and custom error validation messages can also be defined in Mongoose for having more control on how and when certain properties are accepted before they can be saved in the database.

Validation rules are defined in the schema. All schema types have a built-in validator `required` which means it cannot contain `undefined` or `null` values. The `required` validator can be of type `boolean`, a `function`, or an `array`. For example:

```
path: { type: String, required: true }
path: { type: String, required: [true, 'Custom error message'] }
path: { type: String, required: () => true }
```

String schema types have the following built-in validators:

- `enum`: This states that the string can only have the value specified in the `enum` array. For instance:

```
gender: {
type: SchemaTypes.String,
enum: ['male', 'female', 'other'],
}
```

- `match`: This uses `RegExp` to test the value. For instance, to allow values that start with `www`:

```
website: {
type: SchemaTypes.String,
match: /^www/,
}
```

- `maxlength`: This defines the maximum length that a string can have.
- `minlength`: This defines the minimum length that a string can have. For instance, to allow only strings between 5 and 20 characters:

```
name: {
type: SchemaTypes.String,
minlength: 5,
maxlength: 20,
}
```

Number schema types have two built-in validators:

- `min`: This defines the minimum value that a number can have.
- `max`: This defines the maximum value that a number can have. For instance, to allow only numbers between `18` and `100`:

```
age: {
type: String,
min: 18,
max: 100,
}
```

 Undefined values pass all validators without error. If you want to throw an error if a value is `undefined`, do not forget to use the `required` validator to `true`

When built-in validators sometimes do not satisfy your requirements or you wish to perform complex validation rules, you have an option or property called `validate`. This accepts an object that has two properties, `validator` and `message`, that allow us to write custom validators:

```
nickname: {
type: String,
validate: {
validator: function validator(value) {
return /^[a-zA-Z-]$/.test(value)
},
message: '{VALUE} is not a valid nickname.',
},
}
```

Getting ready

In this recipe, you will see how to use custom validation rules to ensure that a certain field matches or fulfils a defined rule. First, ensure that you have MongoDB installed and it's running. As an alternative, if you prefer, a MongoDB DBaaS instance in the cloud will also do. Before you start, create a new `package.json` file with the following code:

```
{
  "dependencies": {
    "mongoose": "5.0.11"
  }
}
```

Then, install the dependencies by opening a Terminal and running:

```
npm install
```

How to do it...

Create a user schema and ensure that all user names are of type string, have a minimum length of six characters, have a maximum length of 20 characters, match a regular expression, and are required:

1. Create a new file named `custom-validation.js`
2. Include the Mongoose NPM module and create a new connection to the database:

```
const mongoose = require('mongoose')
const { connection, Schema } = mongoose
mongoose.connect(
    'mongodb://localhost:27017/test'
).catch(console.error)
```

3. Define a schema including validation rules for the `username` field:

```
const UserSchema = new Schema({
    username: {
        type: String,
        minlength: 6,
        maxlength: 20,
        required: [true, 'user is required'],
        validate: {
            message: '{VALUE} is not a valid username',
            validator: (val) => /^[a-zA-Z]+$/.test(val),
        },
    },
})
```

4. Compile the schema into a model:

```
const User = mongoose.model('User', UserSchema)
```

5. Once a connection with the database is established, create a new document with invalid fields and use the `validateSync` document method to trigger the validation built-in and custom methods:

```
connection.once('connected', async () => {
    try {
        const user = new User()
        let errors = null
        // username field is not defined
        errors = user.validateSync()
        console.dir(errors.errors['username'].message)
        // username contains less than 6 characters
        user.username = 'Smith'
        errors = user.validateSync()
        console.dir(errors.errors['username'].message)
        // RegExp matching
        user.username = 'Smith_9876'
        errors = user.validateSync()
        console.dir(errors.errors['username'].message)
    } catch (error) {
        console.dir(error, { colors: true })
    } finally {
        await connection.close()
    }
})
```

6. Save the file

7. Open a Terminal and run:

    node custom-validation.js

8. On the Terminal, the output should display:

```
'user is required'
'Path `username` (`Smith`) is shorter than the minimum allowed
length (6).'
'Smith_9876 is not a valid username'
```

See also

- Chapter 1, *Introduction to the MERN Stack,* section *Installing NPM Packages*
- Chapter 1, *Introduction to the MERN Stack,* section *Installing MongoDB*

Building a RESTful API to manage users with ExpressJS and Mongoose

In this recipe, you will build a RESTful API that will allow the creation of new users, log in, display user information, and delete a user's profile. Furthermore, you will learn how to build a NodeJS REPL with a client API that you can use to interact with your server's RESTful API.

A **REPL (Read-Eval-Print Loop)** is like an interactive shell where you can execute commands one after another. For instance, the Node.js REPL can be opened by running this command in your terminal:

```
node -i
```

Here, the `-i` flag stands for interactive. Now, you can execute the JavaScript code that gets evaluated piece by piece in a new context.

Getting ready

This recipe will be focused on showing the integration of Mongoose with ExpressJS using what was seen in previous recipes. First, ensure that you have MongoDB installed and it's running. As an alternative, if you prefer, a MongoDB DBaaS instance in the cloud will also do. Before you start, create a new `package.json` file with the following code:

```
{
  "dependencies": {
    "body-parser": "1.18.2",
    "connect-mongo": "2.0.1",
    "express": "4.16.3",
    "express-session": "1.15.6",
    "mongoose": "5.0.11",
    "node-fetch": "2.1.2"
  }
}
```

Then, install the dependencies by opening a Terminal and running this code:

```
npm install
```

How to do it...

Firstly, create a file named `server.js` that will include two middleware functions. One that configures a session and the other that makes sure that there is a connection to the MongoDB before allowing any route to be called. Then, we mount our API routes to a specific path:

1. Create a new file named `server.js`

2. Include the required libraries. Then, initialize a new ExpressJS application and create a connection to MongoDB:

```
const mongoose = require('mongoose')
const express = require('express')
const session = require('express-session')
const bodyParser = require('body-parser')
const MongoStore = require('connect-mongo')(session)
const api = require('./api/controller')
const app = express()
const db = mongoose.connect(
    'mongodb://localhost:27017/test'
).then(conn => conn).catch(console.error)
```

3. Use the `body-parser` middleware to parse the request body as JSON:

```
app.use(bodyParser.json())
```

4. Define an ExpressJS middleware function that will ensure your web application is connected to MongoDB first before allowing next route handlers to be executed:

```
app.use((request, response, next) => {
  Promise.resolve(db).then(
  (connection, err) => (
      typeof connection !== 'undefined'
      ? next()
      : next(new Error('MongoError'))
      )
    )
})
```

5. Configure `express-session` middleware to store sessions in the Mongo database instead of storing in memory:

```
app.use(session({
    secret: 'MERN Cookbook Secrets',
    resave: false,
    saveUninitialized: true,
    store: new MongoStore({
        collection: 'sessions',
        mongooseConnection: mongoose.connection,
    }),
}))
```

6. Mount the API controller to the `"/api"` route:

```
app.use('/users', api)
```

7. Listen on port 1773 for new connections:

```
app.listen(
    1337,
    () => console.log('Web Server running on port 1337'),
)
```

8. Save the file

Then, create a new directory named `api`. Next, create the model or business logic of your application. Define a schema for users with static and instance methods that will allow a user to signup, login, logout, get profile data, change their password, and remove their profile:

1. Create a new file named `model.js` in the `api` directory
2. Include the Mongoose NPM module and also the `crypto` NodeJS module that will be used to generate a hash for the user passwords:

```
const { connection, Schema } = require('mongoose')
const crypto = require('crypto')
```

3. Define the schema:

```
const UserSchema = new Schema({
    username: {
        type: String,
        minlength: 4,
        maxlength: 20,
        required: [true, 'username field is required.'],
        validate: {
            validator: function (value) {
                return /^[a-zA-Z]+$/.test(value)
            },
            message: '{VALUE} is not a valid username.',
        },
    },
    password: String,
})
```

4. Define a static model method for `login`:

```
UserSchema.static('login', async function(usr, pwd) {
    const hash = crypto.createHash('sha256')
        .update(String(pwd))
    const user = await this.findOne()
        .where('username').equals(usr)
        .where('password').equals(hash.digest('hex'))
    if (!user) throw new Error('Incorrect credentials.')
    delete user.password
    return user
})
```

5. Define a static model method for `signup`:

```
UserSchema.static('signup', async function(usr, pwd) {
    if (pwd.length < 6) {
        throw new Error('Pwd must have more than 6 chars')
    }
    const hash = crypto.createHash('sha256').update(pwd)
    const exist = await this.findOne()
        .where('username')
        .equals(usr)
    if (exist) throw new Error('Username already exists.')
    const user = this.create({
        username: usr,
        password: hash.digest('hex'),
    })
    return user
})
```

6. Define a document instance method for `changePass`:

```
UserSchema.method('changePass', async function(pwd) {
    if (pwd.length < 6) {
        throw new Error('Pwd must have more than 6 chars')
    }
    const hash = crypto.createHash('sha256').update(pwd)
    this.password = hash.digest('hex')
    return this.save()
})
```

7. Compile the Mongoose schema into a model and export it:

```
module.exports = connection.model('User', UserSchema)
```

8. Save the file

Finally, define a controller that will transform the request body to actions that our model can understand. Then export it as an ExpressJS router that contains all API paths:

1. Create a new file named `controller.js` in the `api` folder
2. Import `model.js` and initialize a new ExpressJS Route:

```
const express = require('express')
const User = require('./model')
const api = express.Router()
```

3. Define a request handler to check if a user is logged in and another request handler to check if the user is not logged in:

```
const isLogged = ({ session }, res, next) => {
    if (!session.user) res.status(403).json({
        status: 'You are not logged in!',
    })
    else next()
}
const isNotLogged = ({ session }, res, next) => {
    if (session.user) res.status(403).json({
        status: 'You are logged in already!',
    })
    else next()
}
```

4. Define a `post` request method to handle requests to `"/login"` endpoint:

```
api.post('/login', isNotLogged, async (req, res) => {
    try {
        const { session, body } = req
  const { username, password } = body
        const user = await User.login(username, password)
        session.user = {
            _id: user._id,
            username: user.username,
        }
        session.save(() => {
            res.status(200).json({ status: 'Welcome!'})
        })
    } catch (error) {
        res.status(403).json({ error: error.message })
    }
})
```

5. Define a `post` request method to handle requests to `"/logout"` endpoint:

```
api.post('/logout', isLogged, (req, res) => {
    req.session.destroy()
    res.status(200).send({ status: 'Bye bye!' })
})
```

6. Define a `post` request method to handle requests to `"/signup"` endpoint:

```
api.post('/signup', async (req, res) => {
    try {
        const { session, body } = req
        const { username, password } = body
        const user = await User.signup(username, password)
        res.status(201).json({ status: 'Created!'})
    } catch (error) {
        res.status(403).json({ error: error.message })
    }
})
```

7. Define a `get` request method to handle requests to `"/profile"` endpoint:

```
api.get('/profile', isLogged, (req, res) => {
    const { user } = req.session
    res.status(200).json({ user })
})
```

8. Define a `put` request method to handle requests to `"/changepass"` endpoint:

```
api.put('/changepass', isLogged, async (req, res) => {
    try {
        const { session, body } = req
        const { password } = body
        const { _id } = session.user
        const user = await User.findOne({ _id })
        if (user) {
            await user.changePass(password)
            res.status(200).json({ status: 'Pwd changed' })
        } else {
            res.status(403).json({ status: user })
        }
    } catch (error) {
        res.status(403).json({ error: error.message })
    }
})
```

9. Define a delete request method to handle requests to `"/delete"` endpoint:

```
api.delete('/delete', isLogged, async (req, res) => {
    try {
        const { _id } = req.session.user
        const user = await User.findOne({ _id })
        await user.remove()
        req.session.destroy((err) => {
            if (err) throw new Error(err)
            res.status(200).json({ status: 'Deleted!'})
        })
    } catch (error) {
        res.status(403).json({ error: error.message })
    }
})
```

10. Export the route:

```
module.exports = api
```

11. Save the file

Let's test it...

You have built a RESTful API that allows users to subscribe or sign up, log in, log out, get their profile, and delete their profile. These actions can be performed by making HTTP requests to the server. We will build now a small NodeJS REPL and client API that could allow you to interact with your RESTful API server with plain JavaScript functions:

1. Move to the root of your project directory and create a new file named `client-repl.js`.

2. Include the `node-fetch` NPM module that will allow making HTTP request to the server. Include as well, the `repl` and `vm` Node.js modules that will allow you to create an interactive Node.js REPL:

```
const repl = require('repl')
const util = require('util')
const vm = require('vm')
const fetch = require('node-fetch')
const { Headers } = fetch
```

3. Define a variable that will later contain the session ID from the cookie once the user is logged-in. The cookie will be used to allow the server recognize the logged in user for actions such as getting information about your profile or changing password:

```
let cookie = null
```

4. Define a helper function named `query` that will allow to make HTTP requests to the server. The `credentials` options, allows to send and receive cookies from and to the server. We define the `headers` that will tell the server the content type of the request body that will be sent as JSON content:

```
const query = (path, ops) => {
    return fetch(`http://localhost:1337/users/${path}`, {
        method: ops.method,
        body: ops.body,
        credentials: 'include',
        body: JSON.stringify(ops.body),
        headers: new Headers({
            ...(ops.headers || {}),
            cookie,
            Accept: 'application/json',
            'Content-Type': 'application/json',
        }),
    }).then(async (r) => {
        cookie = r.headers.get('set-cookie') || cookie
```

```
            return {
                data: await r.json(),
                status: r.status,
            }
        }).catch(error => error)
    }
```

5. Define a method that will allow users to sign up:

```
const signup = (username, password) => query('/signup', {
    method: 'POST',
    body: { username, password },
})
```

6. Define a method that will allow users to log in:

```
const login = (username, password) => query('/login', {
    method: 'POST',
    body: { username, password },
})
```

7. Define a method that will allow users to log out:

```
const logout = () => query('/logout', {
    method: 'POST',
})
```

8. Define a method that will allow users to get their profile:

```
const getProfile = () => query('/profile', {
    method: 'GET',
})
```

9. Define a method that will allow users to change their password:

```
const changePassword = (password) => query('/changepass', {
    method: 'PUT',
    body: { password },
})
```

10. Define a method that will allow users to delete their profile:

```
const deleteProfile = () => query('/delete', {
    method: 'DELETE',
})
```

11. Use the start method from the REPL exported object to start a new REPL server. We will specify the eval method to execute JavaScript code using the VM module, then, if a Promise is returned, it will wait for the Promise to be resolved before allowing the user to input more commands or type more JavaScript code in the REPL. We will also specify also the writer method that will pretty-print the result of calling the previously defined methods:

```
const replServer = repl.start({
    prompt: '> ',
    ignoreUndefined: true,
    async eval(cmd, context, filename, callback) {
        const script = new vm.Script(cmd)
        const is_raw = process.stdin.isRaw
        process.stdin.setRawMode(false)
        try {
            const res = await Promise.resolve(
                script.runInContext(context, {
                    displayErrors: false,
                    breakOnSigint: true,
                })
            )
            callback(null, res)
        } catch (error) {
            callback(error)
        } finally {
            process.stdin.setRawMode(is_raw)
        }
    },
    writer(output) {
        return util.inspect(output, {
            breakLength: process.stdout.columns,
            colors: true,
            compact: false,
        })
    }
})
```

12. Add the previously defined methods to the context of the REPL server where the JavaScript code will be executed:

```
replServer.context.api = {
    signup,
    login,
    logout,
    getProfile,
    changePassword,
    deleteProfile,
}
```

13. Save the file

Now you can run on a terminal your RESTful API server:

```
node server.js
```

And in a different terminal, run the NodeJS REPL application that you just created:

```
node client-repl.js
```

In the REPL, you can execute JavaScript code and you have also access to the exported methods. For instance, you can execute the following JavaScript code line by line in your REPL:

```
api.signup('John', 'zxcvbnm')
api.login('John', 'zxcvbnm')
api.getProfile()
api.changePassword('newPwd')
api.logout()
api.login('John', 'incorrectPwd')
```

How it works...

Your RESTful API server will accept requests for the following paths:

- POST/users/login: If a username does not exist in the users collection in MongoDB, an error message is sent to the client. Otherwise, it returns a welcome message.
- POST/users/logout: This destroys the session ID.

- `POST/users/signup`: This creates a new username with the defined password. However, an error will be sent to the client if the username or password does not pass the validation. It will also send an error message to the client when the username already exists.
- `GET/users/profile`: If the user is logged in, the user information is sent to the client. Otherwise, an error message is sent to the client.
- `PUT/users/changepass/`: This will change the current logged-in user's password. However, if the user is not logged-in, an error message is sent to the client.
- `DELETE/users/delete`: This will remove a logged-in user's profile from the collection `users` in MongoDB. The session will be destroyed and a confirmation message is sent to the client. If the user is not logged-in, an error message is sent to the client

See also

- `Chapter 1`, *Introduction to MERN Stack*, section *Installing NPM Packages*
- `Chapter 1`, *Introduction to MERN Stack*, section *Installing MongoDB*

4
Real-Time Communication with Socket.IO and ExpressJS

In this chapter, we will cover the following recipes:

- Understanding NodeJS events
- Understanding Socket.IO events
- Working with Socket.IO namespaces
- Defining and joining to Socket.IO rooms
- Writing middleware for Socket.IO
- Integrating Socket.IO with ExpressJS
- Using ExpressJS middleware in Socket.IO

Technical requirements

You will be required to have an IDE, Visual Studio Code, Node.js and MongoDB. You will also need to install Git, in order use the Git repository of this book.

The code files of this chapter can be found on GitHub:
https://github.com/PacktPublishing/MERN-Quick-Start-Guide/tree/master/Chapter04

Check out the following video to see the code in action:
https://goo.gl/xfyDBn

Introduction

Modern web applications usually require real-time communication where data is continuously flowing from client to server and vice versa with (almost) no delay.

The HTML5 WebSocket Protocol was created to fulfill this requirement. WebSocket uses a single TCP connection that is kept open even when the server or client is not sending any data. That means, while a connection between the client and the server exists, data can be sent at any time without having to open a new connection to the server.

Real-time communication has several applications from building chat applications to multi-user games, where the response time is really important.

In this chapter, we will focus on learning how to build a real-time web application using Socket.IO (`https://socket.io`) and understanding the Node.js event-driven architecture.

Socket.IO is one of the most used libraries for implementing real-time communication. Socket.IO uses WebSocket whenever possible but falls-back to other methods when WebSocket is not supported on a specific web browser. Because you probably want to make your application accessible from any web browser, having to work directly with WebSocket may not seem like a good idea.

Understanding Node.js events

Node.js has an event-driven architecture. Most of Node.js' core API is built around `EventEmitter`. This is a Node.js module that allows `listeners` to subscribe to certain named events that can be triggered later by an **emitter**.

You can define your own event emitter easily by just including the events Node.js module and creating a new instance of `EventEmitter`:

```
const EventEmitter = require('events')
const emitter = new EventEmitter()
emitter.on('welcome', () => {
    console.log('Welcome!')
})
```

Then, you can trigger the `welcome` event by using the `emit` method:

```
emitter.emit('welcome')
```

It is actually, pretty simple. One of the advantages is that you can subscribe multiple listeners to the same event, and they will get triggered when the `emit` method is used:

```
emitter.on('welcome', () => {
    console.log('Welcome')
})
emitter.on('welcome', () => {
    console.log('There!')
})
emitter.emit('welcome')
```

The `EventEmitter` API provides several helpful methods that give you more control to handle events. Check the official Node.js documentation to see all information about the API: `https://nodejs.org/api/events.html`.

Getting ready

In this recipe, you will create a class that will extend `EventEmitter`, and which will contain its own instance methods to trigger listeners attached to a specific event. First, create a new project by opening a Terminal and running the following line:

```
npm init
```

How to do it...

Create a class that extends `EventEmitter` and define two instance methods called `start` and `stop`. When the `start` method is called, it will trigger all listeners attached to the `start` event. It will keep the starting time using `process.hrtime`. Then, when the `stop` method is called, it will trigger all listeners attached to the `stop` event passing as an argument the difference in time since the `start` method was called:

1. Create a new file named `timer.js`

2. Include the events NodeJS module:

```
const EventEmitter = require('events')
```

3. Define two constants that we will use to convert the returned value of `process.hrtime` from seconds to nanoseconds and then to milliseconds:

```
const NS_PER_SEC = 1e9
const NS_PER_MS = 1e6
```

4. Define a class named `Timer` with two instance methods:

```
class Timer extends EventEmitter {
    start() {
        this.startTime = process.hrtime()
        this.emit('start')
    }
    stop() {
        const diff = process.hrtime(this.startTime)
        this.emit(
            'stop',
            (diff[0] * NS_PER_SEC + diff[1]) / NS_PER_MS,
        )
    }
}
```

5. Create a new instance of the previously defined class:

```
const tasks = new Timer()
```

6. Attach an event listener to the `start` event that will have a loop that will perform multiplications. Afterwards, it will call the `stop` method:

```
tasks.on('start', () => {
    let res = 1
    for (let i = 1; i < 100000; i++) {
        res *= i
    }
    tasks.stop()
})
```

7. Attach an event listener to the `stop` event that will print the time it took for the event `start` to execute all its attached listeners:

```
tasks.on('stop', (time) => {
    console.log(`Task completed in ${time}ms`)
})
```

8. Call the `start` method to trigger all `start` event listeners:

```
tasks.start()
```

9. Save the file
10. Open a new Terminal and run:

```
node timer.js
```

How it works...

When the `start` method is executed, it keeps the starting time using `process.hrtime`, which returns the current high-resolution real time in an array of two items, where the first item is a number that represents seconds while the second item is another number that represents nanoseconds. Then, it triggers all event listeners attached to the `start` event.

On the other side, when the `stop` method is executed, it uses the result of previously calling `process.hrtime` as an argument to the same function, which returns the difference in time. This is useful to measure the time from when the `start` method was called until the time when the `stop` method was called.

There's more...

A common mistake is to assume that events are called asynchronously. It is true that defined events can be called at any time. However, they are still executed synchronously. Take the following example:

```
const EventEmitter = require('events')
const events = new EventEmitter()
events.on('print', () => console.log('1'))
events.on('print', () => console.log('2'))
events.on('print', () => console.log('3'))
events.emit('print')
```

The outputs for the preceding code will be shown as follows:

```
1
2
3
```

If you have a loop running inside one of your events, the next event won't get called until the previous one finishes executing.

Events can be made asynchronous by simply adding an `async` function as an event listener. By doing so, every function will still be called in order from the first `listener` defined to the last. However, the emitter won't wait for the first `listener` to finish its execution to call the next listener. That means you cannot guarantee that the output will always be in the same order, for instance:

```
events.on('print', () => console.log('1'))
events.on('print', async () => console.log(
    await Promise.resolve('2'))
)
events.on('print', () => console.log('3'))
events.emit('print')
```

The outputs for the preceding code will be shown as follows:

```
1
3
2
```

Asynchronous functions allow us to write non-blocking applications. If implemented correctly, you won't run into problems like this above.

`EventEmitter` instances have a method called `listeners` which when executed, providing an event name as an argument, returns an array of the attached listeners for that specific event. We can use this method in a way to allow `async` functions to be executed in the order they were attached, for instance:

```
const EventEmitter = require('events')
class MyEvents extends EventEmitter {
    start() {
        return this.listeners('logme').reduce(
            (promise, nextEvt) => promise.then(nextEvt),
            Promise.resolve(),
        )
    }
}
const event = new MyEvents()
event.on('logme', () => console.log(1))
event.on('logme', async () => console.log(
    await Promise.resolve(2)
))
event.on('logme', () => console.log(3))
event.start()
```

This will execute and display output in the order they were attached:

```
1
2
3
```

Understanding Socket.IO events

Socket.IO is an event-driven module or library, and, as you probably guessed, is based on `EventEmitter`. Everything in Socket.IO works with events. An event is triggered when a new connection is made to the Socket.IO server and an event can be emitted to send data to the client.

The Socket.IO server API differs from the Socket.IO client API. However, both work with events to send data from client to server and vice versa.

The Socket.IO server events

Socket.IO uses a single TCP connection to a single path. That means, by default, the connection is made to the URL `http[s]://host:port/socket.io`. However, within Socket.IO, it allows you to define **namespaces**. That means, different end-points but the connection will still remain a single URL.

 By default, Socket.IO Server uses the `"/"` or root namespace

You can, of course, define multiple instances and listen to different URLs as well. However, we will assume, for the purpose of this recipe, that only one connection is created.

The Socket.IO namespace has the following events that your application can subscribe to:

- `connect` or `connection`: When a new connection is made, this event is fired. It provides a **socket object** to the listener as the first parameter that represents the new connection with the client

```
io.on('connection', (socket) => {
    console.log('A new client is connected')
})
// Which is the same as:
 io.of('/').on('connection', (socket) => {
    console.log('A new client is connected')
})
```

The Socket.IO socket object has the following events:

- `disconnecting`: This event is emitted when the client is going to be disconnected from the server. It provides to the listener a parameter that specifies the reason for the disconnection

```
socket.on('disconnecting', (reason) => {
    console.log('Disconnecting because', reason)
})
```

- `disconnected`: Similar to the disconnecting event. However, this event is fired after the client has been disconnected from the server:

```
socket.on('disconnect', (reason) => {
    console.log('Disconnected because', reason)
})
```

- `error`: This event is emitted when an error occurs within events

```
socket.on('error', (error) => {
    console.log('Oh no!', error.message)
})
```

- `[eventName]`: A user-defined event that will get fired when the client emits an event with the same name. The client can emit an event providing data in the arguments. On the server, the event will be fired and it will receive the data sent by the client

Socket.IO client events

A client doesn't necessarily need to be a web browser. We could write a Node.js Socket.IO client application as well.

The Socket.IO client events are extensive and give a lot of control over your application:

- `connect`: This event gets fired when there is a successful connection to the server

```
clientSocket.on('connect', () => {
    console.log('Successfully connected to server')
})
```

- `connect_error`: This event is emitted when there is an error when trying to connect or reconnect to the server

```
clientSocket.on('connect_error', (error) => {
    console.log('Connection error:', error)
})
```

- `connect_timeout`: By default, the timeout set before a `connect_error` and `connect_timeout` is emitted is 20 seconds. After this, the Socket.IO client may try to reconnect to the server once again:

```
clientSocket.on('connect_timeout', (timeout) => {
    console.log('Connect attempt timed out after', timeout)
})
```

- `disconnect`: This event is fired when the client is disconnected from the server. An argument is provided specifying the reason of the disconnection:

```
clientSocket.on('disconnect', (reason) => {
    console.log('Disconnected because', reason)
})
```

- `reconnect`: Fired after a successful reconnection attempt. An argument is provided that specifies how many attempts happened before the connection was successful:

```
clientSocket.on('reconnect', (n) => {
    console.log('Reconnected after', n, 'attempt(s)')
})
```

- `reconnect_attempt` or `reconnecting`: This event is emitted when trying to reconnect to the server. An argument is provided specifying the number of current attempts to connect to the server:

```
clientSocket.on('reconnect_attempt', (n) => {
    console.log('Trying to reconnect again', n, 'time(s)')
})
```

- `reconnect_error`: Similar to the `connect_error` event. However, it gets fired only if there is an error when trying to reconnect to the server:

```
clientSocket.on('reconnect_error', (error) => {
    console.log('Oh no, couldn't reconnect!', error)
})
```

- `reconnect_failed`: By the default, the maximum number of attempts is set to `Infinity`. That means, it is unlikely that this event will ever get fired. However, we can specify an option to limit the maximum number of connection attempts. Let's see that later:

```
clientSocket.on('reconnect_failed', (n) => {
console.log('Couldn'nt reconnected after', n, 'times')
})
```

- `ping`: In short, this event gets fired to check if the connection with the server is still alive:

```
clientSocket.on('ping', () => {
    console.log('Checking if server is alive')
})
```

- pong: Fired when a response is received from the server after the event ping is fired. An argument is provided specifying the latency or response time:

```
clientSocket.on('pong', (latency) => {
    console.log('Server responded after', latency, 'ms')
})
```

- error: This event is fired when an error occurs within events:

```
clientSocket.on('error', (error) => {
    console.log('Oh no!', error.message)
})
```

- [eventName]: A user-defined event that gets fired when the event is emitted in the server. The arguments provided by the server will be received by the client.

Getting ready

In this recipe, you will build a Socket.IO server and a Socket.IO client using what you have just learned about events. Before you start, create a new package.json file with the following content:

```
{
  "dependencies": {
    "socket.io": "2.1.0"
  }
}
```

Then, install the dependencies by opening a Terminal and running:

```
npm install
```

How to do it...

A Socket.IO server will be built to respond to a single event named time. When the event is fired, it will get the server's current time and emit another event named "got time?" providing two arguments, the current time and a counter that specifies how many times a request was made.

1. Create a new file named simple-io-server.js

2. Include the Socket.IO module and initialize a new server:

```
const io = require('socket.io')()
```

3. Define the URL path where connections will be made:

```
io.path('/socket.io')
```

4. Use the root or "/" namespace:

```
const root = io.of('/')
```

5. When a new connection is made, initialize a `counter` variable to 0. Then, add a new listener to the `time` event that will increase the `counter` by one, every time there is a new request, and emit the `"got time?"` event that will be later defined on the client side:

```
root.on('connection', socket => {
    let counter = 0
    socket.on('time', () => {
        const currentTime = new Date().toTimeString()
        counter += 1
        socket.emit('got time?', currentTime, counter)
    })
})
```

6. Listen on port `1337` for new connections:

```
io.listen(1337)
```

7. Save the file

Next, build a Socket.IO client that will connect to our server:

1. Create a new file named `simple-io-client.js`
2. Include the Socket.IO client module:

```
const io = require('socket.io-client')
```

3. Initialize a new Socket.IO client providing the server URL and an options object where we will define the path used in the URL where the connections will be made:

```
const clientSocket = io('http://localhost:1337', {
    path: '/socket.io',
})
```

4. Add an event listener to the `connect` event. Then, when a connection is made, using a `for` loop, emit the `time` event 5 times:

```
clientSocket.on('connect', () => {
    for (let i = 1; i <= 5; i++) {
        clientSocket.emit('time')
    }
})
```

5. Add an event listener to the `"got time?"` event that will expect to receive two arguments the time and a counter that specifies how many requests were made to the server, then print on the console:

```
clientSocket.on('got time?', (time, counter) => {
    console.log(counter, time)
})
```

6. Save the file

7. Open a Terminal and run first the Socket.IO server:

    node simple-io-server.js

8. Open another terminal and run the Socket.IO client:

    node simple-io-client.js

How it works...

Everything works with events. Socket.IO allows events to be defined in the server side that the client can emit. On the other side, it also allows to define events in the client side that the server can emit.

When a user-defined event is emitted by the server side, the data is sent to the client. The Socket.IO client checks whether there is a listener for that event first. Then, if there is a listener, it will get triggered. The same thing happens the other way around when a user-defined event is emitted by the client side:

1. An event listener `time` was added in our Socket.IO server's **socket object** which can be emitted by the client side

2. An event listener `"got time?"` was added in our Socket.IO Client which can be emitted by the server side

3. On connection, the client emits the `time` event first
4. Afterwards, the `time` event is fired on the server side which will emit the `"got time?"` event providing two arguments, the current server's `time` and a `counter` that specifies how many times a request was made
5. Then, the `"got time?"` event is fired on the client side receiving two arguments that were provided by the server, the `time` and a `counter`

Working with Socket.IO namespaces

Namespaces are a way of separating the business logic of your application while reusing the same TCP connection or minimizing the need for creating new TCP connections for to implement real-time communication between the server and the client.

Namespaces look pretty similar to ExpressJS' route paths:

```
/home
/users
/users/profile
```

However, as mentioned in previous recipes, these are not related to URLs. By default, a single TCP connection is created at this URL `http[s]://host:port/socket.io`

Reusing the same event names is a good practice when using namespaces. For example, let's suppose that we have a Socket.IO server that we use to emit a `setWelcomeMsg` event when the client emits a `getWelcomeMsg` event:

```
io.of('/en').on('connection', (socket) => {
    socket.on('getWelcomeMsg', () => {
        socket.emit('setWelcomeMsg', 'Hello World!')
    })
})
io.of('/es').on('connection', (socket) => {
    socket.on('getWelcomeMsg', () => {
        socket.emit('setWelcomeMsg', 'Hola Mundo!')
    })
})
```

As you can see, we defined a listener for the event `getWelcomeMsg` in two different namespaces:

- If the client is connected to the English or `/en` namespace, when the `setWelcomeMsg` event is fired, the client will receive `"Hello World!"`
- On the other hand, if the client is connected to the Spanish or `/es` namespace, when the `setWelcomeMsg` event is fired, the client will receive `"Hola Mundo!"`

Getting ready

In this recipe, you will see how to work with two different namespaces that contain the same event names. Before you start, create a new `package.json` file with the following content:

```
{
  "dependencies": {
    "socket.io": "2.1.0"
  }
}
```

Then, install the dependencies by opening a terminal and running:

```
npm install
```

How to do it...

Build a Socket.IO server that will fire a `data` event and send an object containing two properties, `title` and `msg`, that will be used to populate HTML content in the selected language. Use namespaces to separate and send different data according to the language that the client chooses, English or Spanish.

1. Create a new file named `nsp-server.js`
2. Include the Socket.IO npm module and the required modules for creating an HTTP server:

```
const http = require('http')
const fs = require('fs')
const path = require('path')
const io = require('socket.io')()
```

3. Use the `http` module to create a new HTTP server that will serve an HTML file you will create later as a Socket.IO client:

```
const app = http.createServer((req, res) => {
  if (req.url === '/') {
        fs.readFile(
        path.resolve(__dirname, 'nsp-client.html'),
        (err, data) => {
            if (err) {
               res.writeHead(500)
               return void res.end()
            }
             res.writeHead(200)
             res.end(data)
        }
        )
     } else {
        res.writeHead(403)
       res.end()
     }
 })
```

4. Specify the path new connections will be made to:

```
io.path('/socket.io')
```

5. For the `"/en"` namespace, add a new event listener, `getData`, which when fired will emit a `data` event on the client side and send an object including a `title` and a `msg` property in the English language:

```
io.of('/en').on('connection', (socket) => {
   socket.on('getData', () => {
      socket.emit('data', {
        title: 'English Page',
        msg: 'Welcome to my Website',
      })
   })
})
```

6. For the `"/es"` namespace, do the same. However, the object sent to the client will include a `title` and a `msg` property in the Spanish language:

```
io.of('/es').on('connection', (socket) => {
    socket.on('getData', () => {
        socket.emit('data', {
            title: 'Página en Español',
            msg: 'Bienvenido a mi sitio Web',
        })
    })
})
```

7. Listen on port `1337` for new connections and attach Socket.IO to the underlying HTTP server:

```
io.attach(app.listen(1337, () => {
    console.log(
        'HTTP Server and Socket.IO running on port 1337'
    )
}))
```

8. Save the file.

Afterwards, create a Socket.IO client that will connect to our server and populate HTML content based on the data received from the server.

1. Create a new file named `nsp-client.html`
2. First, specify the document type as HTML5. Next to it, add an `html` tag and set the language to English. Inside the `html` tag, include the `head` and `body` tags as well:

```
<!DOCTYPE html>
<html lang="en">
<head>
    <meta charset="UTF-8">
    <title>Socket.IO Client</title>
</head>
<body>
    <!-- code here -->
</body>
</html>
```

3. Inside the `body` tag, add the first three elements: a heading (`h1`) that will contain the title of the content, a `p` tag that will include a message from the server, and a `button` that will be used to switch to a different namespace. Also, include the Socket.IO client library. The Socket.IO server will make the library file available at this URL: http[s]://host:port/socket.io/socket.io.js . Then, also include as well the `babel` standalone library which will transform the code in the next steps into JavaScript code that can run in all browsers:

```
<h1 id="title"></h1>
<section id="msg"></section>
<button id="toggleLang">Get Content in Spanish</button>
 <script src="http://localhost:1337/socket.io/socket.io.js">
 </script>
  <script src="https://unpkg.com/@babel/standalone/babel.min.js">
 </script>
```

4. Inside the `body`, after the last `script` tags, add another `script` tag and set its type to `"text/babel"`:

```
<script type="text/babel">
    // code here!
</script>
```

5. After that, inside the `script` tag, add the following JavaScript code

6. Define three constants that will contain a reference to the elements we have created in the `body`:

```
const title = document.getElementById('title')
const msg = document.getElementById('msg')
const btn = document.getElementById('toggleLang')
```

7. Define a Socket.IO client manager. It will help us to create sockets with the provided configuration:

```
const manager = new io.Manager(
    'http://localhost:1337',
    { path: '/socket.io' },
)
```

8. Create a new socket that will connect to the `"/en"` namespace. We will assume that this is the default connection:

```
const socket = manager.socket('/en')
```

9. Reserve two connections for namespaces "/en" and "/es". A reserved connection will allow us to switch to a different namespace without the need of to create a new TCP connection:

```
manager.socket('/en')
manager.socket('/es')
```

10. Add an event listener that, once the socket is connected, will emit a `getData` event to request data from the server:

```
socket.on('connect', () => {
    socket.emit('getData')
})
```

11. Add an event listener for the `data` event that will get triggered when the client received data from the server:

```
socket.on('data', (data) => {
    title.textContent = data.title
    msg.textContent = data.msg
})
```

12. Add an event listener for the `button`. When it gets clicked, switch to a different namespace:

```
btn.addEventListener('click', (event) => {
    socket.nsp = socket.nsp === '/en'
        ? '/es'
        : '/en'
    btn.textContent = socket.nsp === '/en'
        ? 'Get Content in Spanish'
        : 'Get Content in English'
    socket.close()
    socket.open()
})
```

13. Save the file

14. Open a new terminal and run:

```
node nsp-server.js
```

15. In the web browser, navigate to:

```
http://localhost:1337/
```

Let's test it...

To see your previous work in action, follow these steps:

1. Once you navigate to `http://localhost:1337/` in your web browser, click on the `"Get Content in Spanish"` button to switch to the Spanish namespace

2. Click on the `"Get Content in English"` button to switch back to the English namespace

How it works...

This is what happens on the server side:

1. We defined two namespaces, `"/en"` and `"/es"`, then added a new event listener, `getData`, to the **socket object.**

2. When the `getData` event is fired in any of the two defined namespaces, it will emit a data event and send an object, that contains a title and a message property, to the client

On the client side, inside the script tag in our HTML document:

1. Initially, a new socket is created for the namespace `"/en"`:

```
const socket = manager.socket('/en')
```

2. At the same time, we created two new **sockets** for the namespaces `"/en"` and `"/es"`. They will act as reserved connections:

```
manager.socket('/en')
manager.socket('/es')
```

3. After, an event listener connect was added that sends a request to the server on connection

4. Then, another event listener data was added that is fired when data is received from the server

5. Inside the event listener that handles onclick events for our button, we change the nsp property to switch to a different namespace. However, for this to happen, we had to disconnect the **socket** first, and call the open method to make a new connection again using the new namespace

Let's see one of the confusing parts about reserved connections. When you create one or more **sockets** in the same namespace, the first connection is reused, for example:

```
const first = manager.socket('/home')
const second = manager.socket('/home') // <- reuses first connection
```

On the client side, if there were no reserved connections, then switching to a namespace that was not used before would result in a new connection being created.
If you are curious, remove these two lines from the `nsp-client.html` file:

```
manager.socket('/en')
manager.socket('/es')
```

Afterwards, restart or run the Socket.IO server again. You will notice that there is a slow response when switching to a different namespace because a new connection is created instead of being reused.

There is an alternative way of achieving the same goal. We could have created two sockets that point to two different namespaces, `"/en"` and `"/es"`. Then, we could have added two event listeners connect and data to each socket. However, because the first and second socket would contain the same event names and receive data in the same format from the server, we would have gotten repeated code. Imagine the case if we had to do the same for five different namespaces that have the same event names and receive data in the same format, there would be too many repeated lines of code. This is where switching namespaces and reusing the same socket object is helpful. However, there may be cases were two or more different namespaces have different event names for different kinds of event, in that case, it is better to add event listeners for each of the namespaces separately. For example:

```
const englishNamespace = manager.socket('/en')
const spanishNamespace = manager.socket('/es')
// They listen to different events
englishNamespace.on('showMessage', (data) => {})
spanishNamespace.on('mostrarMensaje', (data) => {})
```

There's more...

On the client side, you have probably noticed one thing that we didn't use before, `io.Manager`.

io.Manager

This allows us predefine or configure how new connections will be created. The options defined in a `Manager`, as the URL, will be passed to the socket on initiation.

In our HTML file, inside a `script` tag, we created a new instance of `io.Manager` and passed two arguments; the server URL and an options object including a `path` property which indicates where new connections will be made:

```
const manager = new io.Manager(
    'http://localhost:1337',
    { path: '/socket.io' },
)
```

To find out more about the `io.Manager` API visit the official documentation Website offer for Socket.IO `https://socket.io/docs/client-api/#manager`.

Later, we used the `socket` method to initialize and create a new Socket for the provided namespace:

```
const socket = manager.socket('/en')
```

This way, it is easier to work with several namespaces at the same time without having to configure each one of them with the same options.

Defining and joining Socket.IO rooms

Within namespaces, you can define rooms or channels that a socket can join and leave.

By default, a room is created with a random un-guessable ID for the connected **socket**:

```
io.on('connection', (socket) => {
    console.log(socket.id) // Outputs socket ID
})
```

On connection, when emitting an event, for example:

```
io.on('connection', (socket) => {
    socket.emit('say', 'hello')
})
```

What happens underneath is similar to this:

```
io.on('connection', (socket) => {
    socket.join(socket.id, (err) => {
        if (err) {
            return socket.emit('error', err)
        }
        io.to(socket.id).emit('say', 'hello')
    })
})
```

The `join` method was used to include the socket inside a room. In this case, the socket ID is the joint room, and the only client connected to that room is the socket itself.

Because a socket ID represents a unique connection with a client and, by default, a room with the same ID is created; all data sent by the server to that room will be received only by that client. However, if several clients or socket IDs join a room with the same name and the server sends data; all clients could be able to receive it.

Getting ready

In this recipe, you will see how to join a room and broadcast a message to all clients connected to that specific room. Before you start, create a new `package.json` file with the following content:

```
{
  "dependencies": {
    "socket.io": "2.1.0"
  }
}
```

Then, install the dependencies by opening a terminal and running:

npm install

How to do it...

Build a Socket.IO server that will notify all the connected clients to the `"commonRoom"` room when a new socket is connected.

1. Create a new file named `rooms-server.js`
2. Include the Socket.IO NPM module and initialize a new HTTP server:

```
const http = require('http')
const fs = require('fs')
const path = require('path')
const io = require('socket.io')()
const app = http.createServer((req, res) => {
    if (req.url === '/') {
        fs.readFile(
            path.resolve(__dirname, 'rooms-client.html'),
            (err, data) => {
                if (err) {
                    res.writeHead(500)
                    return void res.end()
                }
                res.writeHead(200)
                res.end(data)
            }
        )
    } else {
        res.writeHead(403)
        res.end()
    }
})
```

3. Specify the path where new connections will be made:

```
io.path('/socket.io')
```

4. Use the root namespace to listen for events:

```
const root = io.of('/')
```

5. Define a method that will be used to emit an `updateClientCount` event to all socket clients connected to the `"commonRoom"` providing as an argument the number of connected clients:

```
const notifyClients = () => {
    root.clients((error, clients) => {
        if (error) throw error
```

```
        root.to('commonRoom').emit(
            'updateClientCount',
            clients.length,
        )
    })
}
```

6. On connection, all newly connected Socket clients will join the `commonRoom`. Then, the server will emit a `welcome` event. After this, notify all connected sockets to update the number of connected clients and also do the same operation once a client is disconnected:

```
root.on('connection', socket => {
    socket.join('commonRoom')
    socket.emit('welcome', `Welcome client: ${socket.id}`)
    socket.on('disconnect', notifyClients)
    notifyClients()
})
```

7. Listen on port `1337` for new connections and attach Socket.IO to the HTTP server:

```
io.attach(app.listen(1337, () => {
    console.log(
        'HTTP Server and Socket.IO running on port 1337'
    )
}))
```

8. Save the file.

After this, build a Socket.IO client that will connect to the Socket.IO server and populate the HTML content with received data:

1. Create a new file named `rooms-client.html`
2. Add the following code:

```
<!DOCTYPE html>
<html lang="en">
<head>
    <meta charset="UTF-8">
    <title>Socket.IO Client</title>
</head>
<body>
    <h1 id="title">
        Connected clients:
        <span id="n"></span>
```

```
    </h1>
    <p id="welcome"></p>
    <script src="http://localhost:1337/socket.io/socket.io.js">
    </script>
    <script
    src="https://unpkg.com/@babel/standalone/babel.min.js">
    </script>
    <script type="text/babel">
// Code here
    </script>
</body>
</html>
```

3. Inside the script tag, add code in the following steps, starting from step 4

4. Define two constants that will make a reference to two HTML elements that we will update according to the data sent by the Socket.IO Server:

```
const welcome = document.getElementById('welcome')
const n = document.getElementById('n')
```

5. Define a Socket.IO Client Manager:

```
const manager = new io.Manager(
    'http://localhost:1337',
    { path: '/socket.io' },
)
```

6. Use the root namespace which is the one used in the Socket.IO Server:

```
const socket = manager.socket('/')
```

7. Add an event listener for the `welcome` event that expects an argument that will contain a welcome message sent by the server:

```
socket.on('welcome', msg => {
    welcome.textContent = msg
})
```

8. Add an event listener for the `updateClientCount` event that expects an argument that will contain the number of connected clients:

```
socket.on('updateClientCount', clientsCount => {
    n.textContent = clientsCount
})
```

9. Save the file

10. Open a new Terminal and run:

   node rooms-server.js

11. On the web browser, navigate to:

   http://localhost:1337/

12. Without closing the previous tab or window, on the web browser, navigate once again to:

   http://localhost:1337/

13. The number of connected clients in both tabs or windows should have increased to 2

There's more...

Sending the same message or data, to more than one client, is called broadcasting. The method we have seen broadcasts a message to all clients, including the client that generated the request.

There are other several methods to broadcast a message. For instance:

```
socket.to('commonRoom').emit('updateClientCount', data)
```

Which will emit an updateClientCount event to all clients in commonRoom expect to the sender or the socket that originated the request.

For a complete list check the official documentation of Socket.IO emit cheatsheet: https://socket.io/docs/emit-cheatsheet/

Writing middleware for Socket.IO

Socket.IO allows us to define two kinds of middleware functions in the server side:

- **Namespace middleware**: Registers a function that gets executed for every new connected Socket and has the following signature:

   ```
   namespace.use((socket, next) => { ... })
   ```

- **Socket middleware**: Registers a function that gets executed for every incoming Packet and has the following signature:

```
socket.use((packet, next) => { ... })
```

It works similarly to how ExpressJS middleware functions do. We can add new properties to the `socket` or `packet` objects. Then, we can call `next` to pass the control to the next middleware in the chain. If `next` is not called, then the `socket` won't be connected, or the `packet` received.

Getting ready

In this recipe, you will build a Socket.IO server application where you will define middleware functions to restrict access to a certain namespace as well as restricting access to a certain socket based on some criteria. Before you start, create a new `package.json` file with the following content:

```
{
  "dependencies": {
    "socket.io": "2.1.0"
  }
}
```

Then, install the dependencies by opening a terminal and running:

```
npm install
```

How to do it...

The Socket.IO server application will expect the users to be logged-in in order for them to be able to connect to the `/home` namespace. Using socket middleware, we will also restrict access to `/home` namespace to a certain user:

1. Create a new file named `middleware-server.js`
2. Include the Socket.IO library and initialize a new HTTP server:

```
const http = require('http')
const fs = require('fs')
const path = require('path')
const io = require('socket.io')()
const app = http.createServer((req, res) => {
    if (req.url === '/') {
```

```
            fs.readFile(
                path.resolve(__dirname, 'middleware-cli.html'),
                (err, data) => {
                    if (err) {
                        res.writeHead(500)
                        return void res.end()
                    }
                    res.writeHead(200)
                    res.end(data)
                }
            )
        } else {
            res.writeHead(403)
            res.end()
        }
    })
```

2. Specify the path where new connections will be made:

```
io.path('/socket.io')
```

3. Define an array of users that we will use as an in-memory database:

```
const users = [
    { username: 'huangjx', password: 'cfgybhji' },
    { username: 'johnstm', password: 'mkonjiuh' },
    { username: 'jackson', password: 'qscwdvb' },
]
```

4. Define a method to verify if the provided username and password exist in the users array:

```
const userMatch = (username, password) => (
    users.find(user => (
        user.username === username &&
        user.password === password
    ))
)
```

5. Define a namespace middleware function that will check whether the user is already logged-in. A client won't be able to connect to a specific namespace using this middleware if they are not logged in:

```
const isUserLoggedIn = (socket, next) => {
    const { session } = socket.request
    if (session && session.isLogged) {
        next()
```

```
        }
    }
```

6. Define two namespaces, one for /login and another for /home. The /home namespace will use our previously defined middleware function to check whether the user is logged in:

```
const namespace = {
    home: io.of('/home').use(isUserLoggedIn),
    login: io.of('/login'),
}
```

7. When a new socket is connected to /login namespace, first we will define a socket middleware function for checking all incoming packages and ban access to the johntm username. Then, we will add an event listener for the enter event that will expect to receive a plain object containing a username and password, and if they exist in the users array, then we set a session object which will tell whether the user is logged in. Otherwise, we will send a loginError event with an error message to the client:

```
namespace.login.on('connection', socket => {
    socket.use((packet, next) => {
        const [evtName, data] = packet
        const user = data
        if (evtName === 'tryLogin'
            && user.username === 'johnstm') {
            socket.emit('loginError', {
                message: 'Banned user!',
            })
        } else {
            next()
        }
    })
    socket.on('tryLogin', userData => {
        const { username, password } = userData
        const request = socket.request
        if (userMatch(username, password)) {
            request.session = {
                isLogged: true,
                username,
            }
            socket.emit('loginSuccess')
        } else {
            socket.emit('loginError', {
                message: 'invalid credentials',
            })
```

```
        }
    })
})
```

8. Listen on port 1337 for new connections and attach Socket.IO to the HTTP server:

```
io.attach(app.listen(1337, () => {
    console.log(
        'HTTP Server and Socket.IO running on port 1337'
    )
}))
```

9. Save the file

After this, build a Socket.IO client application that will connect to our Socket.IO Server and allow us to attempt to log in and test:

1. Create a new file named `middleware-cli.html`
2. Add the following code:

```html
<!DOCTYPE html>
<html lang="en">
<head>
    <meta charset="UTF-8">
    <title>Socket.IO Client</title>
    <script src="http://localhost:1337/socket.io/socket.io.js">
    </script>
    <script
    src="https://unpkg.com/@babel/standalone/babel.min.js">
    </script>
</head>
<body>
    <h1 id="title"></h1>
    <form id="loginFrm" disabled>
      <input type="text" name="username" placeholder="username"/>
        <input type="password" name="password"
          placeholder="password" />
        <input type="submit" value="LogIn" />
        <output name="logs"></output>
    </form>
    <script type="text/babel">
        // Code here
    </script>
</body>
</html>
```

3. Inside the script tag, add the code in the following steps, starting from step 4

4. Define three constant that will make a reference to the HTML elements that we will use to get input or display output:

```
const title = document.getElementById('home')
const error = document.getElementsByName('logErrors')[0]
const loginForm = document.getElementById('loginForm')
```

5. Define a Socket.IO Manager:

```
const manager = new io.Manager(
    'http://localhost:1337',
    { path: '/socket.io' },
)
```

6. Let's define a namespace constant that will contain an object containing the Socket.IO namespaces /home and /login:

```
const namespace = {
    home: manager.socket('/home'),
    login: manager.socket('/login'),
}
```

7. Add an event listener for the connect event to the /home namespace. It will get triggered only when the /home namespace successfully connects to the server:

```
namespace.home.on('connect', () => {
    title.textContent = 'Great! you are connected to /home'
    error.textContent = ''
})
```

8. Add an event listener for the loginSuccess event to the /login namespace. It will ask the /home namespace to connect to the server again. If the user is logged in, then the server will allow this connection:

```
namespace.login.on('loginSuccess', () => {
    namespace.home.connect()
})
```

9. Add an event listener for the loginError event to the /login namespace. It will display error messages sent by the server:

```
namespace.login.on('loginError', (err) => {
    logs.textContent = err.message
})
```

10. Add an event listener for the submit event for the login form. It will emit the enter event providing an object containing the username and password filled in the form:

```
form.addEventListener('submit', (event) => {
    const body = new FormData(form)
    namespace.login.emit('tryLogin', {
        username: body.get('username'),
        password: body.get('password'),
    })
    event.preventDefault()
})
```

11. Save the file

Let's test it...

To see our previous work in action:

1. Run the Socket.IO server first. Open a new terminal and run:

   node middleware-server.js

2. On your web browser, navigate to:

   http://localhost:1337

3. You will see a login form with two fields, `username` and `password`

4. Try to log in with random invalid credentials. The following error is displayed:

   ```
   invalid credentials
   ```

5. Next, try to log in with `johntm` as `username` and any `password`. The following error is displayed:

   ```
   Banned user!
   ```

6. After that, log in with any of the two other valid credentials. For instance, using `jingxuan` as username and `qscwdvb` as password. The following title is displayed:

   ```
   Connected to /home
   ```

Integrating Socket.IO with ExpressJS

Socket.IO works well with ExpressJS. In fact, it's possible to run an ExpressJS application and a Socket.IO server using the same port or HTTP server.

Getting ready

In this recipe, we will see how to integrate Socket.IO with ExpressJS. You will build an ExpressJS application that will serve an HTML file containing a Socket.IO client application. Before you start, create a new `package.json` file with the following content:

```
{
  "dependencies": {
    "express": "4.16.3",
    "socket.io": "2.1.0"
  }
}
```

Then, install the dependencies by opening a terminal and running:

```
npm install
```

How to do it...

Create a Socket.IO client application that will connect to the Socket.IO server, that you will build next, and display a welcome message sent by the server.

1. Create a new file named `io-express-view.html`
2. Add the following code:

```
<!DOCTYPE html>
<html lang="en">
<head>
    <meta charset="UTF-8">
    <title>Socket.IO Client</title>
    <script src="http://localhost:1337/socket.io/socket.io.js">
    </script>
    <script
     src="https://unpkg.com/@babel/standalone/babel.min.js">
    </script>
</head>
<body>
    <h1 id="welcome"></h1>
```

```
    <script type="text/babel">
        const welcome = document.getElementById('welcome')
        const manager = new io.Manager(
            'http://localhost:1337',
            { path: '/socket.io' },
        )
        const root = manager.socket('/')
        root.on('welcome', (msg) => {
            welcome.textContent = msg
        })
    </script>
</body>
</html>
```

3. Save the file

Next, build an ExpressJS application and a Socket.IO server. The ExpressJS application will serve the previously created HTML file on the root path "/":

1. Create a new file named `io-express-server.js`
2. Initialize a new Socket.IO server application and an ExpressJS application:

```
const path = require('path')
const express = require('express')
const io = require('socket.io')()
const app = express()
```

3. Define the URL path where new connections will be made to the Socket.IO server:

```
io.path('/socket.io')
```

4. Define a route method to serve our HTML file containing our Socket.IO client application:

```
app.get('/', (req, res) => {
    res.sendFile(path.resolve(
        __dirname,
        'io-express-view.html',
    ))
})
```

5. Define a namespace "/" and emit a `welcome` event with welcome message:

```
io.of('/').on('connection', (socket) => {
    socket.emit('welcome', 'Hello from Server!')
})
```

6. Attach the Socket.IO to ExpressJS Server:

```
io.attach(app.listen(1337, () => {
    console.log(
        'HTTP Server and Socket.IO running on port 1337'
    )
}))
```

7. Save the file

8. Open the Terminal and run:

node io-express-server.js

9. In your browser, visit:

```
http://localhost:1337/
```

How it works...

Socket.IO's `attach` method expects to receive a HTTP server as a parameter in order to attach the Socket.IO server application to it. The reason why we can attach Socket.IO to an ExpressJS server application is because the `listen` method returns the underlying HTTP server to which ExpressJS is connected.

To sum up, the `listen` method returns the underlying HTTP server. Then, it is passed as a parameter to the `attach` method. This way, we can share the same connection with ExpressJS.

There's more...

So far, we have seen that we can share the same underlying HTTP server between ExpressJS and Socket.IO. However, that is not all.

The reason why we define a Socket.IO path is actually useful when working with ExpressJS. Take the following example:

```
const express = require('express')
const io = require('socket.io')()
const app = express()
io.path('/socket.io')
 app.get('/socket.io', (req, res) => {
    res.status(200).send('Hey there!')
})
```

```
io.of('/').on('connection', socket => {
    socket.emit('someEvent', 'Data from Server!')
})
io.attach(app.listen(1337))
```

As you can see, we are using the same URL path for Socket.IO and ExpressJS. We accept new connections to the Socket.IO server on the `/socket.io` path, but we also send content for `/socket.io` using the GET route method.

Even though this preceding example won't actually break your application, make sure to never use the same URL path to serve content from ExpressJS and accept new connections for Socket.IO at the same time. For instance, changing the previous code to this:

```
io.path('/socket.io')
 app.get('/socket.io/:msg', (req, res) => {
    res.status(200).send(req.params.msg)
})
```

While you may expect your browser, when visiting `http://localhost:1337/socket.io/message`, to display `message`, that won't be the case and you will see the following instead:

```
{"code":0,"message":"Transport unknown"}
```

That is because Socket.IO will interpret the incoming data first and it won't understand the data you just sent. In addition, your route handler will never be executed.

Besides that, the Socket.IO server also serves, by default, its own Socket.IO Client under the defined URL path. For example, try visiting `http://localhost:1337/socket.io/socket.io.js` and you will be able to see the minimized JavaScript code of the Socket.IO client.

If you wish to server your own version of Socket.IO client or if it is included in the bundle of your application, you can disable the default behavior in your Socket.IO server application with the `serveClient` method:

```
io.serveClient(false)
```

See also

- Chapter 2, *Building a Web server with ExpressJS*, section *Using Express.js' built-in middleware function for serving static assets*

Using ExpressJS middleware in Socket.IO

Socket.IO namespace middleware works pretty similar to how ExpressJS middleware does. In fact, the Socket Object also contains a `request` and a `response` object that we can use to store other properties in the same manner as we do with ExpressJS middleware functions:

```
namespace.use((socket, next) => {
    const req = socket.request
    const res = socket.request.res
    next()
})
```

Because ExpressJS middleware functions have the following signature:

```
const expressMiddleware = (request, response, next) => {
    next()
}
```

We can safely execute the same function in a Socket.IO namespace middleware passing the necessary arguments:

```
root.use((socket, next) => {
    const req = socket.request
    const res = socket.request.res
    expressMiddleware(req, res, next)
})
```

However, that doesn't mean that all ExpressJS middleware functions will work out of the box. For example, if an ExpressJS middleware function uses methods only available within ExpressJS, it may fail or have an unexpected behavior.

Getting ready

In this recipe, we will see how to integrate the ExpressJS `express-session` middleware to share the session object between Socket.IO and ExpressJS. Before you start, create a new `package.json` file with the following content:

```json
{
  "dependencies": {
    "express": "4.16.3",
    "express-session": "1.15.6",
    "socket.io": "2.1.0"
  }
}
```

Then, install the dependencies by opening a Terminal and running:

```
npm install
```

How to do it...

Build a Socket.IO client application that will connect to a Socket.IO server you will build next. Include a form where the user can type a username and a password to attempt to log in. The Socket.IO client will only be able to connect to the `/home` namespace after the user is logged-in:

1. Create a new file named `io-express-cli.html`
2. Add the following HTML content:

```html
<!DOCTYPE html>
<html lang="en">
<head>
    <meta charset="UTF-8">
    <title>Socket.IO Client</title>
    <script src="http://localhost:1337/socket.io/socket.io.js">
    </script>
    <script
     src="https://unpkg.com/@babel/standalone/babel.min.js">
    </script>
</head>
<body>
    <h1 id="title"></h1>
    <form id="loginForm">
      <input type="text" name="username" placeholder="username"/>
        <input type="password" name="password"
```

```
            placeholder="password" />
        <input type="submit" value="LogIn" />
        <output name="logErrors"></output>
    </form>
    <script type="text/babel">
        // Code here
    </script>
</body>
</html>
```

3. Inside the script tag add the code in the next steps, starting from step 4

4. Define constants that make a reference to the HTML elements that we will use:

```
const title = document.getElementById('title')
const error = document.getElementsByName('logErrors')[0]
const loginForm = document.getElementById('loginForm')
```

5. Define a Socket.IO Manager:

```
const manager = new io.Manager(
    'http://localhost:1337',
    { path: '/socket.io' },
)
```

6. Define two namespaces, one for /login and another one for /home:

```
const namespace = {
    home: manager.socket('/home'),
    login: manager.socket('/login'),
}
```

7. Add an event listener for the welcome event that will be triggered by the server side once a connection is allowed to the /home namespace:

```
namespace.home.on('welcome', (msg) => {
    title.textContent = msg
    error.textContent = ''
})
```

8. Add an event listener for loginSuccess event that, when triggered, will ask the /home namespace to try and reconnect to the Socket.IO Server:

```
namespace.login.on('loginSuccess', () => {
    namespace.home.connect()
})
```

9. Add an event listener for `loginError` event that will display an error when invalid credentials are provided:

```
namespace.login.on('loginError', err => {
    error.textContent = err.message
})
```

10. Add an event listener for `submit` event that will get triggered when submitting the form. It will emit an `enter` event with data containing the provided `username` and `password`:

```
loginForm.addEventListener('submit', event => {
    const body = new FormData(loginForm)
    namespace.login.emit('enter', {
        username: body.get('username'),
        password: body.get('password'),
    })
    event.preventDefault()
})
```

11. Save the file.

After this, build an ExpressJS application that will serve the Socket.IO client on the root path `"/"` and a Socket.IO server that will include the logic for logging the user:

1. Create a new file named `io-express-srv.js`

2. Initialize a new ExpressJS application and a Socket.IO server application. Also, include the `express-session` NPM module:

```
const path = require('path')
const express = require('express')
const io = require('socket.io')()
const expressSession = require('express-session')
const app = express()
```

3. Define the path where new connections to Socket.IO server will be made:

```
io.path('/socket.io')
```

4. Define an ExpressJS session middleware function with the given options:

```
const session = expressSession({
    secret: 'MERN Cookbook Secret',
    resave: true,
    saveUninitialized: true,
})
```

5. Define a Socket.IO namespace middleware that will use the previously created session middleware to generate a session object:

```
const ioSession = (socket, next) => {
    const req = socket.request
    const res = socket.request.res
    session(req, res, (err) => {
        next(err)
        req.session.save()
    })
}
```

6. Define two namespaces, one for /home and another for /login:

```
const home = io.of('/home')
const login = io.of('/login')
```

7. Define an in-memory database or array of objects that will contain username and password properties. These define which users are allowed to login:

```
const users = [
    { username: 'huangjx', password: 'cfgybhji' },
    { username: 'johnstm', password: 'mkonjiuh' },
    { username: 'jackson', password: 'qscwdvb' },
]
```

8. Include the session middleware in ExpressJS:

```
app.use(session)
```

9. Add a route method for /home path that will serve our previously created HTML document containing the Socket.IO client:

```
app.get('/home', (req, res) => {
    res.sendFile(path.resolve(
        __dirname,
        'io-express-cli.html',
    ))
})
```

10. Use the session middleware in `/home` Socket.IO namespace. Then, check for every new socket if the user is logged in. If not, forbid the user to connect to this namespace:

```
home.use(ioSession)
home.use((socket, next) => {
    const { session } = socket.request
    if (session.isLogged) {
        next()
    }
})
```

11. Once a connection is made to the `/home` namespace, meaning that the user can log in, emits a `welcome` event with a welcome message that will be displayed to the user:

```
home.on('connection', (socket) => {
    const { username } = socket.request.session
    socket.emit(
        'welcome',
        `Welcome ${username}!, you are logged in!`,
    )
})
```

12. Use the Session Middleware in the `/login` Socket.IO namespace. Then, when the client emits an `enter` event with the provided username and password, it verifies the profile exists in the `users` array. If the user exists, set the `isLogged` property to `true` and the `username` property to the current user that has logged in:

```
login.use(ioSession)
login.on('connection', (socket) => {
    socket.on('enter', (data) => {
        const { username, password } = data
        const { session } = socket.request
        const found = users.find((user) => (
            user.username === username &&
            user.password === password
        ))
        if (found) {
            session.isLogged = true
            session.username = username
            socket.emit('loginSuccess')
        } else {
            socket.emit('loginError', {
                message: 'Invalid Credentials',
```

```
            })
        }
    })
})
```

13. Listen on port `1337` for new connections and attach the Socket.IO server to it:

```
io.attach(app.listen(1337, () => {
    console.log(
        'HTTP Server and Socket.IO running on port 1337'
    )
}))
```

14. Save the file

15. Open a new Terminal and run:

    node io-express-srv.js

16. In your browser, visit:

    `http://localhost:1337/home`

17. Login with valid credentials. For example:

    ```
    * Username: johntm
    * Password: mkonjiuh
    ```

18. If you logged in successfully, after refreshing the page, your Socket.IO client application will still be able to connect to `/home` and you will see a welcome message every time

How it works...

When the session middleware is used inside ExpressJS, after modifying the session object, the `save` method is automatically called at the end of the response. However, that is not the case when using the session middleware in Socket.IO namespaces, that is why we call the `save` method manually to save the session back to the store. In our case, the store is the memory where the sessions are kept until the server stops.

Forbidding access to certain namespaces based on specific conditions is possible thanks to Socket.IO namespace middleware. If the control is not passed to the `next` handler, then the connection is not made. That's why after the login is successful, we ask the `/home` namespace to attempt to connect again.

See also

- Chapter 2, *Building a Web server with ExpressJS*, section *Writing middleware functions*

5
Managing State with Redux

In this chapter, we will cover the following recipes:

- Defining actions and action creators
- Defining reducer functions
- Creating a Redux store
- Binding action creators to the dispatch method
- Splitting and combining reducers
- Writing Redux store enhancers
- Time traveling with Redux
- Understanding Redux middleware
- Dealing with asynchronous data flow

Technical requirements

You will be required to have an IDE, Visual Studio Code, Node.js and MongoDB. You will also need to install Git, in order use the Git repository of this book.

The code files of this chapter can be found on GitHub:
`https://github.com/PacktPublishing/MERN-Quick-Start-Guide/tree/master/Chapter05`

Check out the following video to see the code in action:
`https://goo.gl/mU9AjR`

Introduction

Redux is a predictable state container for JavaScript applications. It allows developers to manage the state of their applications with ease. With Redux, the state is immutable. Thus, it is possible to go back and forth to the next or previous state of your application. Redux is bound to three core principles:

- **Single source of truth**: All the state of your application must be stored in a single object tree within one single store
- **State is read-only**: You must not mutate the state tree. Only by dispatching an action can the state tree change
- **Changes are made with pure functions**: These are called reducers, which are functions that accept the previous state and an action and compute a new state. Reducers must never mutate the previous state but rather always return a new one

Reducers work in a very similar way to how the `Array.prototype.reduce` function does. The `reduce` method executes a function for every item in an array against an accumulator to reduce it to a single value. For example:

```
const a = 5
const b = 10
const c = [a, b].reduce((accumulator, value) => {
    return accumulator + value
}, 0)
```

The resulting value in variable `c` while reducing `a` and `b` against the `accumulator`, is `15` and the initial value is `0`. The reducer function here is:

```
(accumulator, value) => {
    return accumulator + value
}
```

Redux reducers are written in a similar way and they are the most important concept of Redux. For example:

```
const reducer = (prevState, action) => newState
```

In this chapter, we will focus on learning how to manage simple and complex state trees with Redux. You will learn as well how to deal with asynchronous data flows.

Defining actions and action creators

Reducers accept an `action` object that describes the action that is going to be performed and decides how to transform the state based on this `action` object.

Actions are just plain objects and they have only one required property that needs to be present, the action-type. For instance:

```
const action = {
    type: 'INCREMENT_COUNTER',
}
```

We can also provide additional properties as well. For instance:

```
const action = {
    type: 'INCREMENT_COUNTER',
    incrementBy: 2,
}
```

Actions creators are just functions that return actions, for instance:

```
const increment = (incrementBy) => ({
    type: 'INCREMENT_COUNTER',
    incrementBy,
})
```

Getting ready

In this recipe, you will see how these simple Redux concepts can be applied with `Array.prototype.reduce` to decide how data should be accumulated or reduced.

We won't need the Redux library yet for this purpose.

How to do it...

Build a small JavaScript application that will increase or decreased a counter based on the action provided.

1. Create a new file named `counter.js`

2. Define action-types as constants:

```
const INCREMENT_COUNTER = 'INCREMENT_COUNTER'
const DECREMENT_COUNTER = 'DECREMENT_COUNTER'
```

3. Define two action creators for generating two kinds of actions to `increment` and `decrement` the counter:

```
const increment = (by) => ({
    type: INCREMENT_COUNTER,
    by,
})
const decrement = (by) => ({
    type: DECREMENT_COUNTER,
    by,
})
```

4. Initialize the initial accumulator to 0, then reduce it by passing several actions. The reducer function will decide which kind of action to perform based on the action type:

```
const reduced = [
    increment(10),
    decrement(5),
    increment(3),
].reduce((accumulator, action) => {
    switch (action.type) {
        case INCREMENT_COUNTER:
      return accumulator + action.by
        case DECREMENT_COUNTER:
            return accumulator - action.by
        default:
            return accumulator
    }
}, 0)
```

5. Log the resulting value:

```
console.log(reduced)
```

6. Save the file
7. Open a terminal and run:

node counter.js

7. Outputs: 8

How it works...

1. The first action type that the reducer encounters is `increment(10)` which will increment the accumulator by 10. Because the initial value of the accumulator is 0, the next current value will be 10
2. The second action type tells the reducer function to decrement the accumulator by 5. Thus, the accumulator's value will be 5.
3. The last action type tells the reducer function to increment the accumulator by 3. As a result, the accumulator's value will be 8.

Defining reducer functions

Redux reducers are pure functions. That means, they have no side-effects. Given the same arguments, the reducer must always generate the same shape of state. Take for example the following reducer function:

```
const reducer = (prevState, action) => {
    if (action.type === 'INC') {
        return { counter: prevState.counter + 1 }
    }
    return prevState
}
```

If we execute this function providing the same arguments, the result will always be the same:

```
const a = reducer(
    { counter: 0 },
    { type: 'INC' },
) // Value is { counter: 1 }
const b = reducer(
    { counter: 0 },
    { type: 'INC' },
) // Value is { counter: 1 }
```

 However, take into account that even though the returned values have the same shape, these are two different objects. For instance, comparing the above:

`console.log(a === b)` returns false.

Impure reducer functions prevent your application state from being predictable and make difficult to reproduce the same state. For instance:

```
const impureReducer = (prevState = {}, action) => {
    if (action.type === 'SET_TIME') {
        return { time: new Date().toString() }
    }
    return prevState
}
```

If we execute this function:

```
const a = impureReducer({}, { type: 'SET_TIME' })
setTimeout(() => {
    const b = impureReducer({}, { type: 'SET_TIME' })
    console.log(
        a, // Output may be: {time: "22:10:15 GMT+0000"}
        b, // Output may be: {time: "22:10:17 GMT+0000"}
    )
}, 2000)
```

As you can see, after executing the function for a second time after 2 seconds, we get a different result. To make it pure, you can consider re-writing the previously impure reducer as:

```
const timeReducer = (prevState = {}, action) => {
    if (action.type === 'SET_TIME') {
        return { time: action.time }
    }
    return prevState
}
```

Then, you can safely pass a time property inside your action to set the time:

```
const currentTime = new Date().toTimeString()
const a = timeReducer(
    { time: null },
    { type: 'SET_TIME', time: currentTime },
)
const b = timeReducer(
    { time: null },
    { type: 'SET_TIME', time: currentTime },
)
console.log(a.time === b.time) // true
```

This approach makes your state predictable and the state is easy to reproduce. For instance, you could re-create a scenario of how your application will act if you pass the `time` property for any time in morning or afternoon.

Getting ready

Now that you understand the concept of how reducers work, in this recipe, you will build a small application that will act differently according to the state change.

For this purpose, you won't need to install or use the Redux library yet.

How to do it...

Build an application that will remind you what kind of meal you should get according to your local time. Manage all the state of our application in a single object tree. Also provide a way to simulate what the application will display if it's `00:00a.m` or `12:00p.m`:

1. Create a new file named `meal-time.html`.
2. Add the following code:

```
<!DOCTYPE html>
<html lang="en">
<head>
    <meta charset="UTF-8">
    <title>Breakfast Time</title>
    <script
    src="https://unpkg.com/@babel/standalone/babel.min.js">
    </script>
</head>
<body>
    <h1>What you need to do:</h1>
    <p>
        <b>Current time:</b>
        <span id="display-time"></span>
    </p>
        <p id="display-meal"></p>
        <button id="emulate-night">
        Let's pretend is 00:00:00
    </button>
    <button id="emulate-noon">
        Let's pretend is 12:00:00
    </button>
    <script type="text/babel">
        // Add JavaScript code here
    </script>
</body>
</html>
```

3. Inside the script tag add the code defined in the next steps, starting on step 4.
4. Define a variable `state` that will contain all the state tree and later the next state:

```
let state = {
    kindOfMeal: null,
    time: null,
}
```

5. Create a reference to the HTML elements that we will use to display data or add event listeners:

```
const meal = document.getElementById('display-meal')
const time = document.getElementById('display-time')
const btnNight = document.getElementById('emulate-night')
const btnNoon = document.getElementById('emulate-noon')
```

6. Define two action types:

```
const SET_MEAL = 'SET_MEAL'
const SET_TIME = 'SET_TIME'
```

7. Define an action creator for setting the kind of meal the user should have:

```
const setMeal = (kindOfMeal) => ({
    type: SET_MEAL,
    kindOfMeal,
})
```

8. Define an action creator for setting the time:

```
const setTime = (time) => ({
    type: SET_TIME,
    time,
})
```

9. Define a reducer function that will compute a new state when an action is dispatched:

```
const reducer = (prevState = state, action) => {
    switch (action.type) {
        case SET_MEAL:
            return Object.assign({}, prevState, {
                kindOfMeal: action.kindOfMeal,
            })
        case SET_TIME:
            return Object.assign({}, prevState, {
                time: action.time,
            })
        default:
            return prevState
    }
}
```

10. Add a function that we will call when the state changes, so we can update our view:

```
const onStateChange = (nextState) => {
    const comparison = [
        { time: '23:00:00', info: 'Too late for dinner!' },
        { time: '18:00:00', info: 'Dinner time!' },
        { time: '16:00:00', info: 'Snacks time!' },
        { time: '12:00:00', info: 'Lunch time!' },
        { time: '10:00:00', info: 'Branch time!' },
        { time: '05:00:00', info: 'Breakfast time!' },
        { time: '00:00:00', info: 'Too early for breakfast!' },
    ]
    time.textContent = nextState.time
    meal.textContent = comparison.find((condition) => (
        nextState.time >= condition.time
    )).info
}
```

11. Define a dispatch function that will generate a new state tree by passing the current state and an action to the reducer. Then, it will call the `onChangeState` function to notify your application that the state has changed:

```
const dispatch = (action) => {
    state = reducer(state, action)
    onStateChange(state)
}
```

12. Add an event listener for the button that will emulate that the time is `00:00a.m`:

```
btnNight.addEventListener('click', () => {
    const time = new Date('1/1/1 00:00:00')
    dispatch(setTime(time.toTimeString()))
})
```

13. Add an event listener for the button that will emulate that the time is `12:00p.m`:

```
btnNoon.addEventListener('click', () => {
    const time = new Date('1/1/1 12:00:00')
    dispatch(setTime(time.toTimeString()))
})
```

14. Once the script is running, dispatch an action with the current time for the view to update:

```
dispatch(setTime(new Date().toTimeString()))
```

15. Save the file.

Let's test it...

To see your previous work in action:

1. Open the `meal-time.html` file in your web browser. You can do so by double-clicking on the file, or right-clicking on the file and choosing **Open with...**.
2. You should be able to see your current local time and a message stating what kind of meal you should have. For instance, if your local time is `20:42:35 GMT+0800 (CST)`, you should see `Dinner time!`
3. Click on the button `"Let's pretend is 00:00:00"` to see what your application would display if the time was `00:00a.m.`
4. The same way, click on the button `"Let's pretend is 12:00:00"` to see what your application would display if the time was `12:00p.m.`

How it works...

We can summarize our application like the following to understand how it works:

1. Action types `SET_MEAL` and `SET_TIME` were defined.
2. Two action creators were defined:
    1. `setMeal` which generates an action with the `SET_MEAL` action type and a `kindOfMeal` property with the provided argument
    2. `setTime` which generates an action with the `SET_TIME` action type and a `time` property with the provided argument
3. A reducer function was defined:
    1. For the action type `SET_MEAL`, computes a new state with a new `kindOfMeal` property
    2. For the action type `SET_TIME`, computes a new state with a new `time` property

4. We defined a function that will get called when the state tree changes. Inside the function, we updated the view according to the new state.
5. A `dispatch` function was defined that calls the reducer function providing the previous state and an action object to generate a new state.

Creating a Redux store

In the previous recipes, we have seen how to define reducers and actions. We have also seen how to create a dispatch function to dispatch actions for the reducers to update the state. The store is an object that provides a small API to put all of that together.

The redux module exposes the `createStore` method which we can use to create a store. It has the following signature:

```
createStore(reducer, preloadedState, enhancer)
```

The two last arguments are optional. For example, creating a store with a single reducer could look like this:

```
const TYPE = {
    INC_COUNTER: 'INC_COUNTER',
    DEC_COUNTER: 'DEC_COUNTER',
}
const initialState = {
    counter: 0,
}
const reducer = (state = initialState, action) => {
    switch (action.type) {
        case TYPE.INC_COUNTER:
            return { counter: state.counter + 1 }
        case TYPE.DEC_COUNTER:
            return { counter: state.counter - 1 }
        default:
            return state
    }
}
const store = createStore(reducer)
```

Calling `createStore` will expose four methods:

*   `store.dispatch(action)`: Where action is an object that contains at least one property named `type` that specifies the action type
*   `store.getState()`: Returns the whole state tree

- `store.subscribe(listener)`: Where listener is a callback function that will get triggered whenever the state tree changes. Several listeners can be subscribed
- `store.replaceReducer(reducer)`: Replaces the current Reducer function with a new one

Getting ready

In this recipe, you will re-build the application that you built in the previous recipe. However, this time you will use Redux. Before you start, create a new `package.json` file with the following content:

```
{
    "dependencies": {
        "express": "4.16.3",
        "redux": "4.0.0"
    }
}
```

Then, install the dependencies by opening a terminal and running:

```
npm install
```

How to do it...

First, build a small ExpressJS server application whose sole purpose will be to serve an HTML file and the Redux module:

1. Create a new file named `meal-time-server.js`
2. Include the ExpressJS and `path` module and initialize a new ExpressJS Application:

```
const express = require('express')
const path = require('path')
const app = express()
```

3. Serve the Redux library on `/lib` path. Make sure that the path points to the node_modules folder:

```
app.use('/lib', express.static(
    path.join(__dirname, 'node_modules', 'redux', 'dist')
))
```

4. Serve the client application on the root path /:

```
app.get('/', (req, res) => {
    res.sendFile(path.join(
        __dirname,
        'meal-time-client.html',
    ))
})
```

5. Listen for new connections on port 1337:

```
app.listen(
    1337,
    () => console.log('Web Server running on port 1337'),
)
```

6. Save the file

Now, build the client application using Redux following the next steps:

1. Create a new file named meal-time-client.html.
2. Add the following code:

```
<!DOCTYPE html>
<html lang="en">
<head>
    <meta charset="UTF-8">
    <title>Meal Time with Redux</title>
    <script
    src="https://unpkg.com/@babel/standalone/babel.min.js">
    </script>
    <script src="/lib/redux.js"></script>
</head>
<body>
    <h1>What you need to do:</h1>
    <p>
        <b>Current time:</b>
        <span id="display-time"></span>
    </p>
    <p id="display-meal"></p>
    <button id="emulate-night">
        Let's pretend is 00:00:00
    </button>
    <button id="emulate-noon">
        Let's pretend is 12:00:00
    </button>
    <script type="text/babel">
```

```
        // Add JavaScript code here
    </script>
</body>
</html>
```

3. Inside the script tag, add the code for the next steps, starting from step 4.
4. Extract the `createStore` method from the Redux library:

```
const { createStore } = Redux
```

5. Define the initial state of your application:

```
const initialState = {
    kindOfMeal: null,
    time: null,
}
```

6. Keep a reference of the HTML DOM elements that will be used to display the state or interact with the application:

```
const meal = document.getElementById('display-meal')
const time = document.getElementById('display-time')
const btnNight = document.getElementById('emulate-night')
const btnNoon = document.getElementById('emulate-noon')
```

7. Define two action types:

```
const SET_MEAL = 'SET_MEAL'
const SET_TIME = 'SET_TIME'
```

8. Define two action creators:

```
const setMeal = (kindOfMeal) => ({
    type: SET_MEAL,
    kindOfMeal,
})
const setTime = (time) => ({
    type: SET_TIME,
    time,
})
```

9. Define the reducer that will transform the state when SET_TIME and/or SET_TIME action types are dispatched:

```
const reducer = (prevState = initialState, action) => {
    switch (action.type) {
        case SET_MEAL:
```

```
                    return {...prevState,
                        kindOfMeal: action.kindOfMeal,
                    }
                case SET_TIME:
                    return {...prevState,
                        time: action.time,
                    }
                default:
                    return prevState
            }
        }
```

10. Create a new Redux Store:

```
const store = createStore(reducer)
```

11. Subscribe a callback function to the changes of the store. Whenever the store changes this callback will be triggered and it will update the view according to the changes in the store:

```
store.subscribe(() => {
    const nextState = store.getState()
    const comparison = [
        { time: '23:00:00', info: 'Too late for dinner!' },
        { time: '18:00:00', info: 'Dinner time!' },
        { time: '16:00:00', info: 'Snacks time!' },
        { time: '12:00:00', info: 'Lunch time!' },
        { time: '10:00:00', info: 'Brunch time!' },
        { time: '05:00:00', info: 'Breakfast time!' },
        { time: '00:00:00', info: 'Too early for breakfast!' },
    ]
    time.textContent = nextState.time
    meal.textContent = comparison.find((condition) => (
        nextState.time >= condition.time
    )).info
})
```

12. Add an event listener for the `click` event for our button that will dispatch the `SET_TIME` action type to set the time to `00:00:00`:

```
btnNight.addEventListener('click', () => {
    const time = new Date('1/1/1 00:00:00')
    store.dispatch(setTime(time.toTimeString()))
})
```

13. Add an event listener for the `click` event for our button that will dispatch the `SET_TIME` action type to set the time to `12:00:00`:

```
btnNoon.addEventListener('click', () => {
    const time = new Date('1/1/1 12:00:00')
    store.dispatch(setTime(time.toTimeString()))
})
```

14. When the application is first started, dispatch an action to set the time to the current local time:

```
store.dispatch(setTime(new Date().toTimeString()))
```

15. Save the file

Let's test it...

To see the previous work in action:

1. Open a new terminal and run:

   node meal-time-server.js

2. In your web browser, visit:

   `http://localhost:1337/`

3. You should be able to see your current local time and a message stating what kind of meal you should have. For instance, if your local time is `20:42:35 GMT+0800 (CST)`, you should see `Dinner time!`

4. Click on the button `"Let's pretend is 00:00:00"` to see what your application would display if the time was `00:00a.m.`

5. The same way, click on the `"Let's pretend is 12:00:00"` button to see what your application would display if the time was `12:00p.m.`

There's more

You can use the ES6 spread operator instead of `Object.assign` to merge your previous state with the next one, for instance, we re-wrote the reducer function of the previous recipe:

```
const reducer = (prevState = initialState, action) => {
    switch (action.type) {
        case SET_MEAL:
            return Object.assign({}, prevState, {
                kindOfMeal: action.kindOfMeal,
            })
        case SET_TIME:
            return Object.assign({}, prevState, {
                time: action.time,
            })
        default:
            return prevState
    }
}
```

We rewrote it as the following:

```
const reducer = (prevState = initialState, action) => {
    switch (action.type) {
        case SET_MEAL:
            return {...prevState,
                kindOfMeal: action.kindOfMeal,
            }
        case SET_TIME:
            return {...prevState,
                time: action.time,
            }
        default:
            return prevState
    }
}
```

This could make the code more readable.

Binding action creators to the dispatch method

Actions creators are just functions that generate action objects which can later be used to dispatch actions using the `dispatch` method. Take for example the following code:

```
const TYPES = {
    ADD_ITEM: 'ADD_ITEM',
    REMOVE_ITEM: 'REMOVE_ITEM',
}
const actions = {
    addItem: (name, description) => ({
        type: TYPES.ADD_ITEM,
        payload: { name, description },
    }),
    removeItem: (id) => ({
        type: TYPES.REMOVE_ITEM,
        payload: { id },
    })
}
module.exports = actions
```

Later, somewhere in your application, you can dispatch these actions using the `dispatch` method:

```
dispatch(actions.addItem('Little Box', 'Cats'))
dispatch(actions.removeItem(123))
```

However, as you can see, calling the `dispatch` method every time seems like a repeated and unnecessary step. You could simply wrap the action creators around the `dispatch` function itself like this:

```
const actions = {
    addItem: (name, description) => dispatch({
        type: TYPES.ADD_ITEM,
        payload: { name, description },
    }),
    removeItem: (id) => dispatch({
        type: TYPES.REMOVE_ITEM,
        payload: { id },
    })
}
module.exports = actions
```

Even though this seems like a good solution, there is a problem. It means, you would need to create the store first, then define your action creators binding them to the `dispatch` method. In addition, it would be difficult to maintain the action creators in a separate file since they depend on the `dispatch` method to be present. There is a solution provided by the Redux module, a helper method called `bindActionCreators` which accepts two arguments. The first argument is an object with keys, which represent the name of an action creator, and values, which represent a function that returns an action. The second argument is expected to be the `dispatch` function:

```
bindActionCreators(actionCreators, dispatchMethod)
```

This helper method will map all the action creators to the dispatch method. For instance, we could re-write the previous example as the following:

```
const store = createStore(reducer)
const originalActions = require('./actions')
const actions = bindActionCreators(
    originalActions,
    store.dispatch,
)
```

Then, later somewhere in your application, you can call these methods without wrapping them around the `dispatch` method:

```
actions.addItem('Little Box', 'Cats')
actions.removeItem(123)
```

As you can see, our bound action creators look more like regular functions now. In fact, by destructuring the `actions` object, you can use only the methods you need. For instance:

```
const {
    addItem,
    removeItem,
} = bindActionCreators(
    originalActions,
    store.dispatch,
)
```

Then, you can call them like this:

```
addItem('Little Box', 'Cats')
removeItem(123)
```

Getting ready

In this recipe, you will build a simple To-do application and you will use the concepts that you just have learned about binding action creators. First, create a new `package.json` file with the following content:

```
{
    "dependencies": {
        "express": "4.16.3",
        "redux": "4.0.0"
    }
}
```

Then, install the dependencies by opening a Terminal and running:

```
npm install
```

How to do it...

To build your To-do application, for the purpose of this recipe, define only one action creator and use `bindActionCreators` to bind it to the `dispatch` method.

First, build a small ExpressJS application that will serve the HTML file containing the To-do client application which we will build after:

1. Create a new file named `bind-server.js`
2. Add the following code:

```
const express = require('express')
const path = require('path')
const app = express()
app.use('/lib', express.static(
    path.join(__dirname, 'node_modules', 'redux', 'dist')
))
app.get('/', (req, res) => {
    res.sendFile(path.join(
        __dirname,
        'bind-index.html',
    ))
})
app.listen(
    1337,
    () => console.log('Web Server running on port 1337'),
)
```

3. Save the file

Next, build the To-do application in an HTML file:

1. Create a new file named `bind-index.html`.
2. Add the following code:

```html
<!DOCTYPE html>
<html lang="en">
<head>
    <meta charset="UTF-8">
    <title>Binding action creators</title>
    <script
     src="https://unpkg.com/@babel/standalone/babel.min.js">
    </script>
    <script src="/lib/redux.js"></script>
</head>
<body>
    <h1>List:</h1>
    <form id="item-form">
        <input id="item-input" name="item" />
    </form>
    <ul id="list"></ul>
    <script type="text/babel">
        // Add code here
    </script>
</body>
</html>
```

3. Inside the script tag, add the code in the following steps, starting from step 4.
4. Keep a reference to the HTML DOM element that will be used in the application:

```
const form = document.querySelector('#item-form')
const input = document.querySelector('#item-input')
const list = document.querySelector('#list')
```

5. Define the initial state of your application:

```
const initialState = {
    items: [],
}
```

6. Define an action type:

```
const TYPE = {
    ADD_ITEM: 'ADD_ITEM',
}
```

7. Define an action creator:

```
const actions = {
    addItem: (text) => ({
        type: TYPE.ADD_ITEM,
        text,
    })
}
```

8. Define a reducer function that will add a new item to the list whenever the
   ADD_ITEM action type is dispatched. The state will keep only 5 items:

```
const reducer = (state = initialState, action) => {
    switch (action.type) {
        case TYPE.ADD_ITEM: return {
            items: [...state.items, action.text].splice(-5)
        }
        default: return state
    }
}
```

9. Create a store and bind the dispatch function to the action creator:

```
const { createStore, bindActionCreators } = Redux
const store = createStore(reducer)
const { addItem } = bindActionCreators(
    actions,
    store.dispatch,
)
```

10. Subscribe to the store and whenever the state changes add a new item to the list.
    If an item was already defined, we will re-use it instead of creating a new one:

```
store.subscribe(() => {
    const { items } = store.getState()
    items.forEach((itemText, index) => {
        const li = (
            list.children.item(index) ||
            document.createElement('li')
        )
        li.textContent = itemText
        list.insertBefore(li, list.children.item(0))
    })
})
```

11. Add an event listener to the form for the `submit` event. This way, we can get the input value and dispatch an action:

```
form.addEventListener('submit', (event) => {
    event.preventDefault()
    addItem(input.value)
})
```

12. Save the file.

Let's test it...

To see the previous work in action:

1. Open a new Terminal and run:

   node bind-server.js

2. In your browser, visit:

   `http://localhost:1337/`

3. Type something in the input box and press Enter. A new item should appear in the list.
4. Try to add more than five items to the list. The last one displayed will be removed and only five items are kept on the view.

Splitting and combining reducers

As your application grows, you probably wouldn't want to write all the logic for how the state of your application needs to be transformed in a simple reducer function. What you would probably want is to write smaller reducers that specialize in managing independent parts of the state.

Take for example the following reducer function:

```
const initialState = {
    todoList: [],
    chatMsg: [],
}
const reducer = (state = initialState, action) => {
    switch (action.type) {
```

```
        case 'ADD_TODO': return {
            ...state,
            todoList: [
                ...state.todoList,
                {
                    title: action.title,
                    completed: action.completed,
                },
            ],
        }
        case 'ADD_CHAT_MSG': return {
            ...state,
            chatMsg: [
                ...state.chatMsg,
                {
                    from: action.id,
                    message: action.message,
                },
            ],
        }
        default:
            return state
    }
}
```

You have two properties that manage the state of two different parts of an application. One manages the state of a Todo, list while the other manages the Chat messages. You could split this reducer into two reducer functions, where each manages one slice of the state, for instance:

```
const initialState = {
    todoList: [],
    chatMsg: [],
}
const todoListReducer = (state = initialState.todoList, action) => {
    switch (action.type) {
        case 'ADD_TODO': return state.concat([
            {
                title: action.title,
                completed: action.completed,
            },
        ])
        default: return state
    }
}
const chatMsgReducer = (state = initialState.chatMsg, action) => {
    switch (action.type) {
```

```
        case 'ADD_CHAT_MSG': return state.concat([
            {
                from: action.id,
                message: action.message,
            },
        ])
        default: return state
    }
}
```

However, because `createStore` method accepts only one reducer as the first argument, you would need to combine them into a single reducer:

```
const reducer = (state = initialState, action) => {
    return {
        todoList: todoListReducer(state.todoList, action),
        chatMsg: chatMsgReducer(state.chatMsg, action),
    }
}
```

In this way, we are able to split our reducers into smaller reducers that specialize in managing only one slice of the state, and later combine them together into a single reducer function.

Redux provides a helper method named `combineReducers` that allows you to combine reducers in a similar way to what we just did but without having to repeat a lot of code; for instance, we could rewrite the previous way of combining reducers like this:

```
const reducer = combineReducers({
    todoList: todoListReducer,
    chatMsg: chatMsgReducer,
})
```

The `combineReducers` method is a *higher-order reducer* function. It accepts an object mapping specifies keys to a certain slice of the state managed by a specific `reducer` function and returns a new reducer function. If you run the following code, for instance:

```
console.log(JSON.stringify(
    reducer(initialState, { type: null }),
    null, 2,
))
```

You will see that the generated shape of the state looks like this:

```
{
    "todoList": [],
    "chatMsg": [],
}
```

We can try as well if our combined reducers are working and managing only the part of the state assigned to them. For instance:

```
console.log(JSON.stringify(
    reducer(
        initialState,
        {
            type: 'ADD_TODO',
            title: 'This is an example',
            completed: false,
        },
    ),
    null, 2,
))
```

The output should display the generated state as the following:

```
{
    "todoList": [
        {
            "title": "This is an example",
            "completed": false,
        },
    ],
    "chatMsg": [],
}
```

This shows that each reducer is managing only the slice of the state assigned to them.

Getting ready

In this recipe, you will recreate the To-do application as in the pervious recipe. However, you will add other functionalities such as remove and toggle a To-do item. You will define other state of your application that will be managed by separate reducer functions. First, create a new `package.json` file with the following content:

```
{
    "dependencies": {
        "express": "4.16.3",
```

```
        "redux": "4.0.0"
    }
}
```

Then, install the dependencies by opening a Terminal and running:

```
npm install
```

How to do it...

First, build a small ExpressJS server application that will serve the client application and the Redux library installed in `node_modules`:

1. Create a new file named `todo-time.js`
2. Add the following code:

```
const express = require('express')
const path = require('path')
const app = express()
app.use('/lib', express.static(
    path.join(__dirname, 'node_modules', 'redux', 'dist')
))
app.get('/', (req, res) => {
    res.sendFile(path.join(
        __dirname,
        'todo-time.html',
    ))
})
app.listen(
    1337,
    () => console.log('Web Server running on port 1337'),
)
```

3. Save the file

Next, build the To-do client application. Also include a separate reducer to manage state for the current local time and a random lucky number generator:

1. Create a new file named `todo-time.html`
2. Add the following HTML code:

```
<!DOCTYPE html>
<html lang="en">
<head>
    <meta charset="UTF-8">
```

```
        <title>Lucky Todo</title>
        <script
         src="https://unpkg.com/@babel/standalone/babel.min.js">
        </script>
        <script src="/lib/redux.js"></script>
    </head>
<body>
        <h1>List:</h1>
        <form id="item-form">
            <input id="item-input" name="item" />
        </form>
        <ul id="list"></ul>
        <script type="text/babel">
            // Add code here
        </script>
</body>
</html>
```

3. Inside the script tag add the JavaScript code following the next steps, starting from step 4

4. Keep a reference of the HTML elements that we will use to display data or interact with the application:

```
const timeElem = document.querySelector('#current-time')
const formElem = document.querySelector('#todo-form')
const listElem = document.querySelector('#todo-list')
const inputElem = document.querySelector('#todo-input')
const luckyElem = document.querySelector('#lucky-number')
```

5. Get the createStore method and helper methods from the Redux library:

```
const {
    createStore,
    combineReducers,
    bindActionCreators,
} = Redux
```

6. Set action types:

```
const TYPE = {
    SET_TIME: 'SET_TIME',
    SET_LUCKY_NUMBER: 'SET_LUCKY_NUMBER',
    ADD_TODO: 'ADD_TODO',
    REMOVE_TODO: 'REMOVE_TODO',
    TOGGLE_COMPLETED_TODO: 'TOGGLE_COMPLETED_TODO',
}
```

7. Define action creators:

```
const actions = {
    setTime: (time) => ({
        type: TYPE.SET_TIME,
        time,
    }),
    setLuckyNumber: (number) => ({
        type: TYPE.SET_LUCKY_NUMBER,
        number,
    }),
    addTodo: (id, title) => ({
        type: TYPE.ADD_TODO,
        title,
        id,
    }),
    removeTodo: (id) => ({
        type: TYPE.REMOVE_TODO,
        id,
    }),
    toggleTodo: (id) => ({
        type: TYPE.TOGGLE_COMPLETED_TODO,
        id,
    }),
}
```

8. Define a reducer function to manage the slice of state that keeps the time:

```
const currentTime = (state = null, action) => {
    switch (action.type) {
        case TYPE.SET_TIME: return action.time
        default: return state
    }
}
```

9. Define a reducer function to manage the slice of state that keeps a lucky number that will be generated every time the user loads your application:

```
const luckyNumber = (state = null, action) => {
    switch (action.type) {
        case TYPE.SET_LUCKY_NUMBER: return action.number
        default: return state
    }
}
```

10. Define a reducer function to manage the slice of state that keeps an array of To-do items:

```
const todoList = (state = [], action) => {
    switch (action.type) {
        case TYPE.ADD_TODO: return state.concat([
            {
                id: String(action.id),
                title: action.title,
                completed: false,
            }
        ])
        case TYPE.REMOVE_TODO: return state.filter(
            todo => todo.id !== action.id
        )
        case TYPE.TOGGLE_COMPLETED_TODO: return state.map(
            todo => (
                todo.id === action.id
                    ? {
                        ...todo,
                        completed: !todo.completed,
                    }
                    : todo
            )
        )
        default: return state
    }
}
```

11. Combine all reducers into a single one:

```
const reducer = combineReducers({
    currentTime,
    luckyNumber,
    todoList,
})
```

12. Create a store:

```
const store = createStore(reducer)
```

13. Bind all actions creators to the `dispatch` method of the store:

```
const {
    setTime,
    setLuckyNumber,
    addTodo,
    removeTodo,
    toggleTodo,
} = bindActionCreators(actions, store.dispatch)
```

14. Subscribe a listener to the store that will update the HTML element, that will hold the time, whenever the state changes:

```
store.subscribe(() => {
    const { currentTime } = store.getState()
    timeElem.textContent = currentTime
})
```

15. Subscribe a listener to the store that will update the HTML element, that will display a lucky number, whenever the state changes:

```
store.subscribe(() => {
    const { luckyNumber } = store.getState()
    luckyElem.textContent = `Your lucky number is: ${luckyNumber}`
})
```

16. Subscribe a listener to the store that will update the HTML element that will display the list of To-do items, whenever the state changes. Set the attribute `draggable` for the `li` HTML elements to allow the user to drag and drop the items on the view:

```
store.subscribe(() => {
    const { todoList } = store.getState()
    listElem.innerHTML = ''
    todoList.forEach(todo => {
        const li = document.createElement('li')
        li.textContent = todo.title
        li.dataset.id = todo.id
        li.setAttribute('draggable', true)
        if (todo.completed) {
            li.style = 'text-decoration: line-through'
        }
        listElem.appendChild(li)
    })
})
```

17. Add an event listener for the `click` event on the list HTML element that will toggle a To-do item's `completed` property whenever the item is clicked:

```
listElem.addEventListener('click', (event) => {
    toggleTodo(event.target.dataset.id)
})
```

18. Add an event listener for the `drag` event on the list HTML element that will remove a To-do Item when this one is dragged outside of the list:

```
listElem.addEventListener('drag', (event) => {
    removeTodo(event.target.dataset.id)
})
```

19. Add an event listener for the `submit` event on the form that contains an input HTML element that will dispatch a new action to add a new To-do item:

```
let id = 0
formElem.addEventListener('submit', (event) => {
    event.preventDefault()
    addTodo(++id, inputElem.value)
    inputElem.value = ''
})
```

20. When the page loads for the first time, dispatch an action to set a lucky number and define a function that will get triggered every second to update the current time in the state of the application:

```
setLuckyNumber(Math.ceil(Math.random() * 1024))
setInterval(() => {
    setTime(new Date().toTimeString())
}, 1000)
```

21. Save the file

Let's test it...

To see the previous work in action:

1. Open a new Terminal and run:

`node todo-time.js`

2. In your browser, visit:

   ```
   http://localhost:1337/
   ```

3. Introduce something in the input box and press enter. A new item should appear in the list.
4. Click on one of the items that you have added to mark it as completed.
5. Click once again on one of the items marked as completed to mark it as not completed.
6. Click and drag one of the items outside of the list to remove it from the To-do list.

How it works...

1. Three reducer functions were defined to independently manage each slice of the state that has the following shape:

   ```
   {
       currentTime: String,
       luckyNumber: Number,
       todoList: Array.of({
           id: Number,
           title: String,
           completed: Boolean,
       }),
   }
   ```

2. We used the `combineReducers` helper method from the Redux library to combine those three reducers into a single one
3. Then, a store was created providing the combined reducer function
4. For convenience, we subscribed three listener functions that get triggered whenever the state changes to update the HTML elements used to display the data from the state
5. We also defined three event listeners: one to detect when a user submits a form that contains an input HTML element to add a new To-do item, another to detect when the user clicks on a To-do item displayed on the screen to toggle its state from not completed to completed or vice versa, and finally one event listener to detect when the user drags an element from the list to dispatch an action to remove it from the list of To-do items

Writing Redux store enhancers

A Redux store enhancer is a higher-order function that takes a store creator function and returns a new enhanced store creator function. The createStore method is a store creator which has the following signature:

```
createStore = (reducer, preloadedState, enhancer) => Store
```

While a store enhancer function has the following signature:

```
enhancer = (...optionalArguments) => (
createStore => (reducer, preloadedState, enhancer) => Store
)
```

It may look a bit difficult to understand now, but you don't really have to worry if you don't get it at first because you will probably never need to write a store enhancer. The purpose of this recipe was simply to help you to understand their purpose in a very simple way.

Getting ready

In this recipe, you will create a store enhancer to expand the functionality of Redux by allowing the definition of reducer functions in a Map JavaScript native object. First, create a new package.json file with the following content:

```
{
    "dependencies": {
        "redux": "4.0.0"
    }
}
```

Then, install the dependencies by opening a Terminal and running:

```
npm install
```

How to do it...

Remember that `createStore` accepts a single reducer function as the first argument. We write a store enhancer to allow the `createStore` method to accept a `Map` object containing key-value pairs, where key is the property or slice of state that will be managed, and value is a `reducer` function. Then, define two reducer functions using a `Map` object to handle two slices of the state, one for a counter and the other for setting the current time:

1. Create a new file named `map-store.js`.
2. Include the Redux library:

```
const {
    createStore,
    combineReducers,
    bindActionCreators,
} = require('redux')
```

3. Define a store enhancer function that will allow the `createStore` method to accept a `Map` object as an argument. It will go through each key-value pair of the `Map` and add it to an object which will then be used to combine the reducers using the `combineReducers` method:

```
const acceptMap = () => createStore => (
    (reducerMap, ...rest) => {
        const reducerList = {}
        for (const [key, val] of reducerMap) {
            reducerList[key] = val
        }
        return createStore(
            combineReducers(reducerList),
            ...rest,
        )
    }
)
```

4. Define actions types:

```
const TYPE = {
    INC_COUNTER: 'INC_COUNTER',
    DEC_COUNTER: 'DEC_COUNTER',
    SET_TIME: 'SET_TIME',
}
```

5. Define actions creators:

```
const actions = {
    incrementCounter: (incBy) => ({
        type: TYPE.INC_COUNTER,
        incBy,
    }),
    decrementCounter: (decBy) => ({
        type: TYPE.DEC_COUNTER,
        decBy,
    }),
    setTime: (time) => ({
        type: TYPE.SET_TIME,
        time,
    }),
}
```

6. Define a `map` constant that will contain an instance of `Map`:

```
const map = new Map()
```

7. Add a new reducer function to the `map` object with a key `counter`:

```
map.set('counter', (state = 0, action) => {
    switch (action.type) {
        case TYPE.INC_COUNTER: return state + action.incBy
        case TYPE.DEC_COUNTER: return state - action.decBy
        default: return state
    }
})
```

8. Add another reducer function to the `map` object with a key `time`:

```
map.set('time', (state = null, action) => {
    switch (action.type) {
        case TYPE.SET_TIME: return action.time
        default: return state
    }
})
```

9. Create a new store providing the `map` as the first argument and the **store enhancer** as the second argument to extend the functionality of the `createStore` method:

```
const store = createStore(map, acceptMap())
```

10. Bind the previously defined actions creators to the `dispatch` method of the store:

```
const {
    incrementCounter,
    decrementCounter,
    setTime,
} = bindActionCreators(actions, store.dispatch)
```

11. To test the code in NodeJS, use the `setInterval` global method to repeatedly call a function every second. It will first dispatch an action to set the current time, then, based on the criteria, it will decide if to increment or decrement the counter. After, pretty print in the terminal the current value of the store:

```
setInterval(function() {
    setTime(new Date().toTimeString())
    if (this.shouldIncrement) {
        incrementCounter((Math.random() * 5) + 1 | 0)
    } else {
        decrementCounter((Math.random() * 5) + 1 | 0)
    }
    console.dir(
        store.getState(),
        { colors: true, compact: false },
    )
    this.shouldIncrement = !this.shouldIncrement
}.bind({ shouldIncrement: false }), 1000)
```

12. Save the file.

13. Open a new Terminal and run:

node map-store.js

14. The current state would be displayed every second having this shape:

```
{
    "counter": Number,
    "time": String,
}
```

How it works...

The enhancer composes the store creator into a new one. For instance, the following line:

```
const store = createStore(map, acceptMap())
```

Could be written as:

```
const store = acceptMap()(createStore)(map)
```

Which actually, in a way, wraps the original `createStore` method into another `createStore` method.

Composition can be explained as a set of functions that are called accepting the result argument of the previous function. For instance:

```
const c = (...args) => f(g(h(...args)))
```

This composes functions `f`, `g`, and `h` from right to left into a single function `c`. That means, we could write the previous line of code also like this:

```
const _createStore = acceptMap()(createStore)
const store = _createStore(map)
```

Here `_createStore` is the result of composing `createStore` and your store enhancer function.

Time traveling with Redux

Even though, you may probably never need to write store enhancers, there is one special that you may find very useful for debugging your Redux powered applications to time travel through the state of your application. You can enable time traveling on your application by simple installing **Redux DevTools Extension** (for Chrome and Firefox): https://github.com/zalmoxisus/redux-devtools-extension.

Getting ready

In this recipe, we will see an example of how to take advanced of this feature and analyze how the state of your application has changed over the time that was running on the browser. First, create a new `package.json` file with the following content:

```
{
    "dependencies": {
        "express": "4.16.3",
        "redux": "4.0.0"
    }
}
```

Then, install the dependencies by opening a Terminal and running:

```
npm install
```

Make sure to have installed the Redux DevTools Extension in your web browser.

How to do it...

Build a counter application that will randomly increment or decrement the initial specified counter 10 times when the application is run on the browser. However, because it happens fast, the user won't be able to notice that the state has actually changed 10 times since the application started. We will use the Redux DevTools Extension to navigate and analyze how the state has changed over time.

First, build a small ExpressJS server application that will serve the client application and the Redux library installed in `node_modules`:

1. Create a new file named `time-travel.js`
2. Add the following code:

```
const express = require('express')
const path = require('path')
const app = express()
app.use('/lib', express.static(
    path.join(__dirname, 'node_modules', 'redux', 'dist')
))
app.get('/', (req, res) => {
    res.sendFile(path.join(
        __dirname,
        'time-travel.html',
    ))
```

```
})
app.listen(
    1337,
    () => console.log('Web Server running on port 1337'),
)
```

3. Save the file

Next, build your counter, Redux powered application, with time travel capabilities:

1. Create a new file named `time-travel.html`
2. Add the following HTML code:

```
<!DOCTYPE html>
<html lang="en">
<head>
    <meta charset="UTF-8">
    <title>Time travel</title>
    <script
     src="https://unpkg.com/@babel/standalone/babel.min.js">
    </script>
    <script src="/lib/redux.js"></script>
</head>
<body>
    <h1>Counter: <span id="counter"></span></h1>
    <script type="text/babel">
        // Add JavaScript Code here
    </script>
</body>
</html>
```

3. Inside the script tag add the JavaScript code that follows the next steps, starting from step 4
4. Keep a reference to the `span` HTML element that will display the current value of the counter whenever the state changes:

```
const counterElem = document.querySelector('#counter')
```

5. Get the `createStore` method and `bindActionCreators` method from the Redux library:

```
const {
    createStore,
    bindActionCreators,
} = Redux
```

6. Define two action types:

```
const TYPE = {
    INC_COUNTER: 'INC_COUNTER',
    DEC_COUNTER: 'DEC_COUNTER',
}
```

7. Define two action creators:

```
const actions = {
    incCounter: (by) => ({ type: TYPE.INC_COUNTER, by }),
    decCounter: (by) => ({ type: TYPE.DEC_COUNTER, by }),
}
```

8. Define a reducer function that will transform the state according to the given action type:

```
const reducer = (state = { value: 5 }, action) => {
    switch (action.type) {
        case TYPE.INC_COUNTER:
            return { value: state.value + action.by }
        case TYPE.DEC_COUNTER:
            return { value: state.value - action.by }
        default:
            return state
    }
}
```

9. Create a new store providing a store enhancer function that will be available on the `window` object when the Redux DevTools extension is installed:

```
const store = createStore(
    reducer,
    (
        window.__REDUX_DEVTOOLS_EXTENSION__ &&
        window.__REDUX_DEVTOOLS_EXTENSION__()
    ),
)
```

10. Bind the action creators to the `dispatch` method of the store:

```
const {
    incCounter,
    decCounter,
} = bindActionCreators(actions, store.dispatch)
```

11. Subscribe a listener function to the store that will update the `span` HTML element whenever the state changes:

```
store.subscribe(() => {
    const state = store.getState()
    counterElem.textContent = state.value
})
```

12. Let's create a `for` loop that will update increment or decrement the counter randomly 10 times when the application is run:

```
for (let i = 0; i < 10; i++) {
    const incORdec = (Math.random() * 10) > 5
    if (incORdec) incCounter(2)
    else decCounter(1)
}
```

13. Save the file

Let's test it...

To see the previous work in action:

1. Open a new Terminal and run:

   node todo-time.js

2. In your Browser, visit:

   http://localhost:1337/

3. Open **Developer Tools** of your Browser and look for the **Redux** tab. You should see a tab like this:

Redux DevTools – Tab Window

4. The slider allows you to move from the last state to the very first state of your application. Try moving the slider to a different position:

Redux DevTools – Moving Slider

5. While moving the slider, you would be able to see in your browser the counters initial value and how it changed those ten times in the for loop

There's more

Redux DevTools has some features that you will probably find amazing and helpful for debugging and managing the state of your application. In fact, if you followed the previous recipes, I suggest you go back to the projects we wrote and enable this enhancer and try to experiment with Redux DevTools.

One of many features of Redux DevTools is the **Log monitor**, which displays in chronological order which action was dispatched and the resulting value of transforming the state:

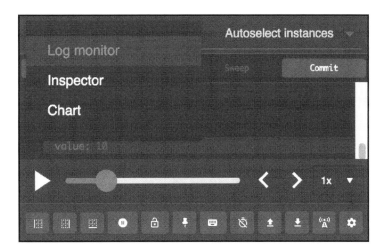

Redux DevTools – Log Monitor

Understanding Redux middleware

Probably the easiest and best way of extending the Redux functionality is by using middleware.

There is a store enhancer function that comes in the Redux library named `applyMiddleware` and allows you define one or multiple middleware functions. The way middleware works in Redux is simple, it allows you to wrap the `dispatch` method of the store to extend its functionality. The same way as store enhancer functions, middleware is composable and has the following signature:

```
middleware = API => next => action => next(action)
```

Here, API is an object containing the `dispatch` and `getState` methods from the store, destructuring the API, the signature looks like this:

```
middleware = ({
    getState,
    dispatch,
}) => next => action => next(action)
```

Let's analyze how it works:

1. The `applyMiddleware` function receives one or more middleware functions as arguments. For example:

   ```
   applyMiddleware(middleware1, middleware2)
   ```

2. Each middleware function is kept internally as an `Array`. Then, internally using the `Array.prototype.map` method, the array maps each middleware function by calling itself providing the middleware API object which contains the `dispatch` and `getState` methods of the store. Similar to this:

   ```
   middlewares.map((middleware) => middleware(API))
   ```

3. Then, by composing all the middleware functions, it computes a new value for the `dispatch` method providing the `next` argument. In the very first middleware that is executed, the `next` argument refers to the original `dispatch` method before any middleware was applied. For instance, if applying three middleware functions, the new computed dispatch method's signature would be:

   ```
   dispatch = (action) => (
       (action) => (
           (action) => store.dispatch(action)
       )(action)
   )(action)
   ```

4. Which means that a middleware function can interrupt the chain and prevent a certain action from being dispatched if the `next(action)` method is not called

5. The dispatch method from the middleware API object, allows you to call the dispatch method of the store with the previously applied middleware. That means, if you are not careful while using this method, you may create an infinite loop

Understanding how it works internally may not be so simple at first, but I assure you that you will get it soon.

Getting ready

In this recipe, you will write a middleware function that will warn the user when dispatching an action type that has not been defined. First, create a new `package.json` file with the following content:

```
{
    "dependencies": {
        "redux": "4.0.0"
    }
}
```

Then, install the dependencies by opening a Terminal and running:

```
npm install
```

How to do it...

Redux doesn't warn you or display errors when an action type, that was never defined within your reducers, is used. Build a NodeJS application that will use Redux to manage its state. Focus on writing a middleware function that will check that the dispatched actions types are defined or else throw an error:

1. Create a new file named `type-check-redux.js`.
2. Include the Redux library:

```
const {
    createStore,
    applyMiddleware,
} = require('redux')
```

3. Define an object containing the allowed action types:

```
const TYPE = {
    INCREMENT: 'INCREMENT',
    DECREMENT: 'DECREMENT',
    SET_TIME: 'SET_TIME',
}
```

4. Create a dummy reducer function that returns its original state whichever action type is called. We don't need it for the purpose of this recipe:

```
const reducer = (
    state = null,
    action,
) => state
```

5. Define a middleware function that will intercept every action that is being dispatched and check whether the action type exists in the TYPE object. If the action exists allow the action to be dispatched, or otherwise, throw an error and inform the user that an invalid action type was dispatched. Additionally, let's provide the user, as part of the error message, information about which valid types are allowed:

```
const typeCheckMiddleware = api => next => action => {
    if (Reflect.has(TYPE, action.type)) {
        next(action)
    } else {
        const err = new Error(
            `Type "${action.type}" is not a valid` +
            `action type. ` +
            `did you mean to use one of the following` +
            `valid types? ` +
            `"${Reflect.ownKeys(TYPE).join('"|"')}"\n`,
        )
        throw err
    }
}
```

6. Create a store and apply the defined middleware function:

```
const store = createStore(
    reducer,
    applyMiddleware(typeCheckMiddleware),
)
```

7. Dispatch two action types. The first action type is valid, and it exists in the TYPE object. However, the second one is an action type that was never defined:

```
store.dispatch({ type: 'INCREMENT' })
store.dispatch({ type: 'MISTAKE' })
```

8. Save the file.

Let's test it...

First, open a new Terminal and run:

```
node type-check-redux.js
```

The Terminal output should display an error similar to this:

```
/type-check-redux.js:25
            throw err
            ^
Error: Type "MISTAKE" is not a valid action type. did you mean to use one
of the following valid types? "INCREMENT"|"DECREMENT"|"SET_TIME"
    at Object.action [as dispatch] (/type-check-redux.js:18:15)
    at Object.<anonymous> (/type-check-redux.js:33:7)
```

In this example, the stack trace tells us that the error happened on line 18, which points to our middleware function. However, the next one points to line 33, `store.dispatch({ type: 'MISTAKE' })`, which is a good thing because it can help you track exactly where certain actions are dispatched that were never defined.

How it works...

It's pretty simple, the middleware function checks the action type, of the action being dispatched, to see if it exists as a property of the `TYPE` object constant. If it exists, then the middleware passes control to the next middleware in the chain. However, in our case, there is no next middleware, so the control is passed to the original dispatch method of the store that will apply the reducer and transform the state. On the other side, if the action type was not defined, the middleware function interrupts the middleware chain by not calling the `next` function and by throwing an error.

Dealing with asynchronous data flow

By default, Redux doesn't handle asynchronous data flow. There are several libraries out there that can help you with these tasks. However, for the purpose of this chapter, we will build our own implementation using middleware functions to give the `dispatch` method the ability to dispatch and handle asynchronous data flow.

Getting ready

In this recipe, you will build an ExpressJS application with a very small API to test your application when making HTTP requests and dealing with asynchronous data flow and errors. First, create a new `package.json` file with the following content:

```
{
    "dependencies": {
        "express": "4.16.3",
        "node-fetch": "2.1.2",
        "redux": "4.0.0"
    }
}
```

Then install the dependencies by opening a Terminal and running:

```
npm install
```

How to do it...

Build a simple RESTful API server that will have two endpoints or answer to paths `/time` and `/date` when a GET request is made. However, on `/date` path, we will pretend that there is an internal error and make the request fail in order to see how to handle errors in asynchronous requests as well:

1. Create a new file named `api-server.js`
2. Include the ExpressJS library and initialize a new ExpressJS application:

```
const express = require('express')
const app = express()
```

3. For `/time` path, simulates a delay of 2s before sending a response:

```
app.get('/time', (req, res) => {
    setTimeout(() => {
        res.send(new Date().toTimeString())
    }, 2000)
})
```

4. For /date path, simulates a delay of 2s before sending a failed response:

```
app.get('/date', (req, res) => {
    setTimeout(() => {
        res.destroy(new Error('Internal Server Error'))
    }, 2000)
})
```

5. Listen on port 1337 for new connections

```
app.listen(
    1337,
    () => console.log('API server running on port 1337'),
)
```

6. Save the file

As for the client, build a NodeJS application using Redux that will dispatch synchronous and asynchronous actions. Write a middleware function to allow the dispatch method to handle asynchronous actions:

1. Create a new file named async-redux.js
2. Include the node-fetch and Redux libraries:

```
const fetch = require('node-fetch')
const {
    createStore,
    applyMiddleware,
    combineReducers,
    bindActionCreators,
} = require('redux')
```

3. Define three kinds of status. Each status represents the state of an asynchronous operation:

```
const STATUS = {
    PENDING: 'PENDING',
    RESOLVED: 'RESOLVED',
    REJECTED: 'REJECTED',
}
```

4. Define two action types:

```
const TYPE = {
    FETCH_TIME: 'FETCH_TIME',
    FETCH_DATE: 'FETCH_DATE',
}
```

5. Define action creators. Notice that the value property is an asynchronous function in the first two action creators. Your, later defined, middleware function will be responsible for making Redux understand these actions:

```
const actions = {
    fetchTime: () => ({
        type: TYPE.FETCH_TIME,
        value: async () => {
            const time = await fetch(
                'http://localhost:1337/time'
            ).then((res) => res.text())
            return time
        }
    }),
    fetchDate: () => ({
        type: TYPE.FETCH_DATE,
        value: async () => {
            const date = await fetch(
                'http://localhost:1337/date'
            ).then((res) => res.text())
            return date
        }
    }),
    setTime: (time) => ({
        type: TYPE.FETCH_TIME,
        value: time,
    })
}
```

6. Define a common function for setting values from an action object that will be used in your reducer:

```
const setValue = (prevState, action) => ({
    ...prevState,
    value: action.value || null,
    error: action.error || null,
    status: action.status || STATUS.RESOLVED,
})
```

7. Define the initial state of your application:

```
const iniState = {
    time: {
        value: null,
        error: null,
        status: STATUS.RESOLVED,
    },
    date: {
        value: null,
        error: null,
        status: STATUS.RESOLVED,
    }
}
```

8. Define a reducer function. Notice that it is only one reducer that handles two slices of the state, the `time` and the `date`:

```
const timeReducer = (state = iniState, action) => {
    switch (action.type) {
        case TYPE.FETCH_TIME: return {
            ...state,
            time: setValue(state.time, action)
        }
        case TYPE.FETCH_DATE: return {
            ...state,
            date: setValue(state.date, action)
        }
        default: return state
    }
}
```

9. Define a middleware function that will check whether a dispatched action type has a function as the `value` property. If that is so, assume that the `value` property is an async function. First, we dispatch an action to set the status as PENDING. Then, when the async function is resolved, we dispatch another action to set the status as RESOLVED or in case of an error as REJECTED:

```
const allowAsync = ({ dispatch }) => next => action => {
    if (typeof action.value === 'function') {
        dispatch({
            type: action.type,
            status: STATUS.PENDING,
        })
        const promise = Promise
            .resolve(action.value())
            .then((value) => dispatch({
```

```
                    type: action.type,
                    status: STATUS.RESOLVED,
                    value,
            }))
                .catch((error) => dispatch({
                    type: action.type,
                    status: STATUS.REJECTED,
                    error: error.message,
            }))
        return promise
    }
    return next(action)
}
```

10. Create a new store and apply your defined middleware function to extend the functionality of the `dispatch` method:

```
const store = createStore(
    timeReducer,
    applyMiddleware(
        allowAsync,
    ),
)
```

11. Bind action creators to the `dispatch` method of the store:

```
const {
    setTime,
    fetchTime,
    fetchDate,
} = bindActionCreators(actions, store.dispatch)
```

12. Subscribe a function listener to the store and display in terminal the state tree, as a JSON string, every time there is a change in the state:

```
store.subscribe(() => {
    console.log('x1b[1;34m%sx1b[0m', 'State has changed')
    console.dir(
        store.getState(),
        { colors: true, compact: false },
    )
})
```

13. Dispatch a synchronous action to set the time:

```
setTime(new Date().toTimeString())
```

14. Dispatch an asynchronous action to fetch and set the time:

```
fetchTime()
```

15. Dispatch another asynchronous action to fetch and try to set the date. Remember that this operation is supposed to fail and it's intentional:

```
fetchDate()
```

16. Save the file.

Let's test it...

To see your previous work in action:

1. Open a new terminal and run:

```
node api-server.js
```

2. Without closing the previously running NodeJS process, open another Terminal and run:

```
node async-redux.js
```

How it works...

1. Every time there is a change in the state, the subscribed listener function will pretty print in the terminal the current state tree
2. The first dispatched action is synchronous. It will cause the time slice of the state tree to be updated like this, for example:

```
time: {
    value: "01:02:03 GMT+0000",
    error: null,
    status: "RESOLVED"
}
```

3. The second action being dispatched is asynchronous. Internally, two actions are dispatched to reflect the state of the asynchronous operation, one when the async function is still in execution, and another when the async function was fulfilled:

```
time: {
    value: null,
    error: null,
    status: "PENDING"
}
// Later, once the operation is fulfilled:
time: {
    value: "01:02:03 GMT+0000",
    error: null,
    status: "RESOLVED"
}
```

4. The third action being dispatched is also asynchronous. Internally, it also causes two actions to be dispatched to reflect the state of the async operation:

```
date: {
    value: null,
    error: null,
    status: "PENDING"
}
// Later, once the operation is fulfilled:
date: {
    value: null,
    error: "request to http://localhost:1337/date failed, reason:
        socket hang up",
    status: "REJECTED"
}
```

5. Take into account that because the operations are asynchronous, the output displayed in the terminal may not always be in the same order

6. Notice that the first async operation is fulfilled and the status marked as RESOLVED while the second async operation is fulfilled and its status marked as REJECTED

7. The statuses PENDING, RESOLVED, and REJECTED reflect the three statuses that a JavaScript Promise can be, and they are not obligatory names, simply easy to remember

There's more...

If you don't want to write your own middleware functions or store enhancers to deal with asynchronous operations, you can opt to use one of the many libraries for Redux that exist out there. Two of the most use or popular ones are these:

- Redux Thunk—https://github.com/gaearon/redux-thunk
- Redux Saga—https://github.com/redux-saga/redux-saga

Building Web Applications with React

6

In this chapter, we will cover the following recipes:

- Understanding React elements and React components
- Composing components
- Stateful components and life cycle methods
- Working with React.PureComponent
- React event handlers
- Conditional rendering of components
- Rendering lists with React
- Working with forms and inputs in React
- Understanding refs and how to use them
- Understanding React portals
- Catching errors with error boundary components
- Type checking properties with PropTypes

Technical requirements

You will be required to know Go programming language, also basics of web application framework. You will also need to install Git, in order use the Git repository of this book. And finally, ability to develop with an IDE on the command line.

The code files of this chapter can be found on GitHub:
`https://github.com/PacktPublishing/MERN-Quick-Start-Guide/tree/master/Chapter06`

Check out the following video to see the code in action:
`https://goo.gl/J7d7Ag`

Introduction

React is a JavaScript library for building **user interfaces** (UI). React is component-based, which means that each component can live separately from others and manage its own state. Complex UIs can be created by composing components.

Components are usually created using JSX syntax, which has an XML-like syntax, or using the `React.createElement` method. However, JSX is what makes React special for building web applications in a declarative way.

 In the MVC pattern, React is usually associated with the View.

Understanding React elements and React components

React elements can be created using JSX syntax:

```
const element = <h1>Example</h1>
```

This is transformed to:

```
const element = React.createElement('h1', null, 'Example')
```

JSX is a language extension on top of JavaScript that allows you to create complex UIs with ease. For example, consider the following:

```
const element = (
    <details>
        <summary>React Elements</summary>
        <p>JSX is cool</p>
    </details>
)
```

The previous example could be written without JSX syntax as:

```
const element = React.createElement(
    'details',
    null,
    React.createElement('summary', null, 'React Elements'),
    React.createElement('p', null, 'JSX is cool'),
)
```

React elements can be any HTML5 tag and any JSX tag can be self-closed. For instance, the following will create a paragraph React element with an empty content within:

```
const element = <p />
```

The same way as you would do with HTML5, you can provide attributes to React elements, called properties or props in React:

```
const element = (
    <input type="text" value="Example" readOnly />
)
```

React components allow you to isolate parts of your web application as re-usable pieces of code or components. They can be defined in several ways. For instance:

- **Functional components**: These are plain JavaScript functions that accept properties as the first argument and return React elements:

```
const InputText = ({ name, children }) => (
    <input
        type="text"
        name={name}
        value={children}
        readOnly
    />
)
```

- **Class components**: Using ES6 classes allows you to define life cycle methods and create stateful components. They render React elements from the `render` method:

```
class InputText extends React.Component {
    render() {
        const { name, children } = this.props
        return (
            <input
                type="text"
                name={name}
```

```
                    value={children}
                    readOnly
              />
           )
        }
    }
```

- **Expressions**: These keep a reference to an instance of a React element or component:

```
const InstanceInputText = (
    <InputText name="username">
        Huang Jx
    </InputText>
)
```

There are a few properties that are unique and are only part of React. For instance, the `children` property refers to the elements contained within the tag:

```
<MyComponent>
    <span>Example</span>
</MyComponent>
```

The `children` property received in `MyComponent`, in the previous example, will be an instance of a `span` React element. If multiple React elements or components are passed as children, the `children` property will be an array. However, if no children are passed, the `children` property will be `null`. The `children` property doesn't necessarily need to be a React element or component; it can also be a JavaScript function, or a JavaScript primitive:

```
<MyComponent>
    {() => {
        console.log('Example!')
        return null
    }}
</MyComponent>
```

React also considers functional components and class components that return or render a string, a valid React component. For instance:

```
const SayHi = ({ to }) => (
    `Hello ${to}`
)
const element = (
    <h1>
        <SayHi to="John" />, how are you?
    </h1>
)
```

React components' names must start with an uppercase letter. Otherwise, React will treat lowercased JSX tags as React elements

Rendering components to the DOM in React is not a complicated task. React provides several methods for rendering a React component to the DOM using the ReactDOM library. React uses JSX or React.createElement to create a tree or a representation of the DOM tree. It does so by using a virtual DOM, which allows React to transform React elements to DOM nodes and update only the nodes that have changed.

This is how you usually render your application using the render method from the ReactDOM library:

```
import * as ReactDOM from 'react-dom'
import App from './App'
ReactDOM.render(
    <App />,
    document.querySelector('[role="main"]'),
)
```

The first argument provided to the render method is a React component or a React element. The second argument tells you where in the DOM to render the application. In the previous example, we use the querySelector method from the document object to look for a DOM node with an attribute of role set to "main".

React also allows you to render React components as an HTML string, which is useful for generating content on the server side and sending the content directly to the browser as an HTML file:

```
import * as React from 'react'
import * as ReactDOMServer from 'react-dom/server'
const OrderedList = ({ children }) => (
    <ol>
        {children.map((item, indx) => (
            <li key={indx}>{item}</li>
        ))}
    </ol>
)
console.log(
    ReactDOMServer.renderToStaticMarkup(
        <OrderedList>
            {['One', 'Two', 'Three']}
        </OrderedList>
    )
```

)

It will output the following in the console:

```
<ol>
    <li>One</li>
    <li>Two</li>
    <li>Three</li>
</ol>
```

Getting ready

In this recipe, you will create a simple React application using the concepts that you have learned about React components and React elements. Before you start, create a new `package.json` file with the following content:

```
{
  "scripts": {
    "start": "parcel serve -p 1337 index.html"
  },
  "devDependencies": {
    "babel-plugin-transform-class-properties": "6.24.1",
    "babel-preset-env": "1.6.1",
    "babel-preset-react": "6.24.1",
    "babel-core": "6.26.3",
    "parcel-bundler": "1.8.1",
    "react": "16.3.2",
    "react-dom": "16.3.2"
  }
}
```

Next, create a babel configuration file as `.babelrc`, adding the following content:

```
{
    "presets": ["env","react"],
    "plugins": ["transform-class-properties"]
}
```

Then, install the dependencies by opening a Terminal and running:

npm install

How to do it...

Create a React application that will display a welcome message writing functional, class, and expression components:

1. Create a new file named `basics.js`.

2. Import the React and ReactDOM libraries:

```
import * as React from 'react'
import * as ReactDOM from 'react-dom'
```

3. Define a new functional component that will render a `span` React element with `color` set to red in its style attributes:

```
const RedText = ({ text }) => (
    <span style={{ color: 'red' }}>
        {text}
    </span>
)
```

4. Define another functional component that will render an `h1` React element and the `RedText` functional component as part of its `children`:

```
const Welcome = ({ to }) => (
    <h1>Hello, <RedText text={to}/></h1>
)
```

5. Define an expression that will contain a reference to a React element:

```
const TodoList = (
    <ul>
        <li>Lunch at 14:00 with Jenny</li>
        <li>Shower</li>
    </ul>
)
```

6. Define a class component named `Footer` that will display the current date:

```
class Footer extends React.Component {
    render() {
        return (
            <footer>
                {new Date().toDateString()}
            </footer>
        )
    }
}
```

7. Render the application to the DOM:

```
ReactDOM.render(
    <div>
        <Welcome to="John" />
        {TodoList}
        <Footer />
    </div>,
    document.querySelector('[role="main"]'),
)
```

8. Save the file.

Then, create an `index.html` file where you will render the React application:

1. Create a new file named `index.html`
2. Add the following code:

```
<!DOCTYPE html>
<html lang="en">
<head>
    <meta charset="UTF-8">
    <title>MyApp</title>
</head>
<body>
    <div role="main"></div>
    <script src="./basics.js"></script>
</body>
</html>
```

3. Save the file

Let's test it...

To see the previous work in action:

1. Open a Terminal at the root of your project directory and run:

   npm start

2. Then, open a new tab in your web browser and go to:

   `http://localhost:1337/`

3. You should be able to see the React application rendered to the DOM

Composing components

In React, all components can be isolated and complex UIs can be built by composing components which enables their re-usability.

Getting ready

In this recipe, you will work with re-usable components to generate a home page containing three sections: a header, a paragraph with a description, and a footer. These three sections will be written as three separate components that will be composed later to build a home page. Before you start, create a new `package.json` file with the following content:

```
{
  "scripts": {
    "start": "parcel serve -p 1337 index.html"
  },
  "devDependencies": {
    "babel-plugin-transform-class-properties": "6.24.1",
    "babel-preset-env": "1.6.1",
    "babel-preset-react": "6.24.1",
    "babel-core": "6.26.3",
    "parcel-bundler": "1.8.1",
    "react": "16.3.2",
    "react-dom": "16.3.2"
  }
}
```

Next, create a babel configuration file as `.babelrc`, adding the following content:

```
{
    "presets": ["env","react"],
    "plugins": ["transform-class-properties"]
}
```

Then, install the dependencies by opening a Terminal and running:

```
npm install
```

How to do it...

Create a new folder named `component` in the root directory of your project. Then, create the following three files in order:

1. `Header.js`
2. `Footer.js`
3. `Description.js`

The `Header` component will generate an `h1` React element that represents the heading of the page. It expects to receive a `title` property:

1. Create a new file named `Header.js` in the `component` directory
2. Add the following code:

    ```
    import * as React from 'react'
    import * as ReactDOM from 'react-dom'
    export default ({ title }) => (
        <h1>{title}</h1>
    )
    ```

3. Save the file

The `Footer` component will generate a `footer` React element that will be placed at the end of the page. It will expect to receive a `date` property:

1. Create a new file named `Footer.js` in the `component` directory
2. Add the following code:

```
import * as React from 'react'
import * as ReactDOM from 'react-dom'
export default ({ date }) => (
    <footer>{date}</footer>
)
```

3. Save the file

The `Description` component will generate a paragraph that will display a description of the page:

1. Create a new file named `Description.js` in the `component` directory
2. Add the following code:

```
import * as React from 'react'
import * as ReactDOM from 'react-dom'
export default () => (
    <p>This is a cool website designed with ReactJS</p>
)
```

3. Save the file

Next, move back out of the `component` directory to the root directory of your project where `package.json` is located and create the following file:

1. Create a new file named `composing-react.js`
2. Import the React and `ReactDOM` libraries:

```
import * as React from 'react'
import * as ReactDOM from 'react-dom'
```

3. Import the previously defined components:

```
import Header from './component/Header'
import Footer from './component/Footer'
import Description from './component/Description'
```

4. Define a `App` component that will render your previously defined components:

```
const App = () => (
    <React.Fragment>
        <Header title="Simple React App" />
        <Description />
        <Footer date={new Date().toDateString()} />
    </React.Fragment>
)
```

5. Render the application:

```
ReactDOM.render(
    <App />,
    document.querySelector('[role="main"]'),
)
```

6. Save the file

Then, create an `index.html` file where you will render the React application:

1. Create a new file named `index.html`
2. Add the following code:

```
<!DOCTYPE html>
<html lang="en">
<head>
    <meta charset="UTF-8">
    <title>Composing Components</title>
</head>
<body>
    <div role="main"></div>
    <script src="./composing-react.js"></script>
</body>
</html>
```

3. Save the file

Let's test it...

To see the previous work in action, perform the following steps:

1. Open a Terminal at the root of your project directory and run:

   npm start

2. Then, open a new tab in your web browser and go to:

```
http://localhost:1337/
```

3. If you inspect the DOM tree in your browser's developer tools, you should be able to see the following DOM structure:

```
<div role="app">
<h1>React App</h1>
<p>This is a cool website designed with ReactJS</p>
<footer>Tue May 22 2018</footer>
</div>
```

How it works...

Each React component is written in a separate file. Then, we import the components in the main application file, `composing-react.js`, and use composition to generate a virtual DOM tree. Each component is re-usable because it can be used again in other parts of your application or in other components by just importing the files. Then, the `render` method from the `ReactDOM` library is used to generate a DOM representation of the virtual DOM tree.

There's more...

Did you notice that we used `React.Fragment`? This is a new feature introduced in React v16. It allows you to return multiple elements without creating an extra DOM node. A component cannot return multiple React components or elements in the following way:

```
const Example = () => (
    <span>One</span>
    <span>Two</span>
) // < will trow an error
```

However, using `React.Fragment`, it's possible to do the following:

```
const Example = () => (
    <React.Fragment>
        <span>One</span>
        <span>Two</span>
    </React.Fragment>
)
```

Stateful components and life cycle methods

React components can manage their own state and update only when the state has
changed. Stateful React components are written using ES6 classes:

```
class Example extends React.Component {
    render() {
        <span>This is an example</span>
    }
}
```

React class components have a `state` instance property to access their internal state and a
`props` property to access properties passed to the component:

```
class Example extends React.Component {
    state = { title: null }
    render() {
        return (
            <React.Fragment>
                <span>{this.props.title}</span>
                <span>{this.state.title}</span>
            </React.Fragment>
        )
    }
}
```

And their state can be mutated by using the `setState` instance method:

```
class Example extends React.Component {
    state = {
        title: "Example",
        date: null,
    }
    componentDidMount() {
        this.setState((prevState) => ({
            date: new Date().toDateString(),
        }))
    }
    render() {
        return (
            <React.Fragment>
                <span>{this.state.title}</span>
                <span>{this.state.date}</span>
            </React.Fragment>
        )
    }
}
```

The state is initialized once. Then, when the component is mounted, the state should only be mutated using the `setState` method. This way, React is able to detect changes in the state and update the component.

The `setState` method accepts a callback function as the first argument which will be executed passing the current state (`prevState` for convention) as the first argument to the callback function and the current `props` as the second argument. This is so because `setState` works asynchronously and the state could be mutated while you are performing other actions in different parts of your component.

If you don't need access to the current state while updating the state, you can directly pass an object as the first argument. For instance, the previous example could have been written as:

```
componentDidMount() {
    this.setState({
        date: new Date().toDateString(),
    })
}
```

`setState` also accepts an optional callback function as a second argument that gets called once the state has been updated. Because `setState` is asynchronous, you may want to use the second callback to perform an action only once the state has been updated:

```
componentDidMount() {
    this.setState({
        date: new Date().toDateString(),
    }, () => {
        console.log('date has been updated!')
    })
    console.log(this.state.date) // null
}
```

Once the component is mounted, the console will first output `null` even though we used `setState` before it; that's because the state is set asynchronously. However, once the state is updated, the console will display "date has been updated".

 When using the `setState` method, React merges the previous state with the current given state. Internally, it's similar to doing:

```
currentState = Object.assign({}, currentState, nextState)
```

Every class component has *life cycle methods* that give you control over the life of your component since its creation until it's destroyed, as well as giving you control over other properties, such as knowing when the component has received new properties and if the component should be updated or not. These are the life cycle methods present in all class components:

- `constructor(props)`: This is invoked when initializing a new instance of the component, before the component is mounted. `props` must be passed to the super class using `super(props)` to let React set the `props` correctly. The `constructor` method is useful as well to initialize the initial state of the component.

- `static getDerivedStateFromProps(nextProps, nextState)`: This is invoked when the component has been instantiated and when the component will receive new `props`. This method is useful when the state or part of it depends on values received from the `props` passed to the component. It must return an object which will be merged with the current state or `null` if the state doesn't need to be updated after receiving new `props`.

- `componentDidMount()`: This is invoked after the component has been mounted and after the first `render` call. It's useful for integrating with third-party libraries, accessing the DOM, or making HTTP requests to an endpoint.

- `shouldComponentUpdate(nextProps, nextState)`: This is invoked when the component has updated the state or new props have been received. This method allows React to know if it should update the component or not. If you don't implement this method in your component, it defaults to returning `true`, which means the component should be updated every time the state has changed or new props have been received. If implementing this method and returning `false`, it will tell React not to update the component.

- `componentDidUpdate(prevProps, prevState, snapshot)`: This is invoked after the render method or when an update occurs, except for the first rendering.

- `getSnapshotBeforeUpdate(prevProps, prevState)`: This is invoked after the render method or when an update occurs but before the `componentDidUpdate` life cycle method. The returned value of this method is passed as the third argument of `componentDidUpdate`.

- `componentWillUnmount()`: This is invoked before a component is unmounted and its instance destroyed. If using third-party libraries, this method is helpful for cleaning up. For instance, clearing timers or cancelling network requests.

- `componentDidCatch(error, info)`: This is a new feature of React v16 for error handling. We will look at this in more detail in the following recipes.

Getting ready

In this recipe, you will build a component using all the life cycle methods that we have learned about. First, create a new `package.json` file with the following content:

```
{
  "scripts": {
    "start": "parcel serve -p 1337 index.html"
  },
  "devDependencies": {
    "babel-plugin-transform-class-properties": "6.24.1",
    "babel-preset-env": "1.6.1",
    "babel-preset-react": "6.24.1",
    "babel-core": "6.26.3",
    "parcel-bundler": "1.8.1",
    "react": "16.3.2",
    "react-dom": "16.3.2"
  }
}
```

Next, create a babel configuration file as `.babelrc`, adding the following content:

```
{
    "presets": ["env","react"],
    "plugins": ["transform-class-properties"]
}
```

Then, install the dependencies by opening a Terminal and running:

```
npm install
```

How to do it...

Build a `LifeCycleTime` component whose only purpose would be to display the current time. The component will be updated every 100 ms to keep the component in sync with the time change. We will use the life cycle methods in this component for the following purposes:

- `constructor(props)`: To initialize the component's initial state.
- `static getDerivedStateFromProps(nextProps, nextState)`: To merge the `props` with the state.
- `componentDidMount()`: To set a function that will be executed every 100 ms using `setInterval`, which will update the state with the current time.

- shouldComponentUpdate(nextProps, nextState):To decide if the component should be rendered or not. Check if props have a property dontUpdate set to true, which means the component shouldn't be updated on a state or props change.
- componentDidUpdate(prevProps, prevState, snapshot): To simply log in the console that the component has been updated displaying the snapshot's value.
- getSnapshotBeforeUpdate(prevProps, prevState): To illustrate the functionality of this method, simply return a string that will be passed as the third argument to componentDidUpdate.
- componentWillUnmount(): When the component is destroyed or unmounted, clear the interval defined in componentDidMount. Otherwise, after the component is unmounted, you will see an error being displayed.

First, create an index.html file where you will render the React application:

1. Create a new file named index.html
2. Add the following code:

```
<!DOCTYPE html>
<html lang="en">
<head>
    <meta charset="UTF-8">
    <title>Life cycle methods</title>
</head>
<body>
    <div role="main"></div>
    <script src="./stateful-react.js"></script>
</body>
</html>
```

3. Save the file

Next, perform the following steps to build the LifeCycleTime component:

1. Create a new file named stateful-react.js
2. Import the React and ReactDOM libraries:

```
import * as React from 'react'
import * as ReactDOM from 'react-dom'
```

3. Define a `LifeCycleTime` class component and use the life cycle methods as previously described:

```
class LifeCycleTime extends React.Component {
    constructor(props) {
        super(props)
        this.state = {
            time: new Date().toTimeString(),
            color: null,
            dontUpdate: false,
        }
    }
    static getDerivedStateFromProps(nextProps, prevState) {
        return nextProps
    }
    componentDidMount() {
        this.intervalId = setInterval(() => {
            this.setState({
                time: new Date().toTimeString(),
            })
        }, 100)
    }
    componentWillUnmount() {
        clearInterval(this.intervalId)
    }
    shouldComponentUpdate(nextProps, nextState) {
        if (nextState.dontUpdate) {
            return false
        }
        return true
    }
    getSnapshotBeforeUpdate(prevProps, prevState) {
        return 'snapshot before update'
    }
    componentDidUpdate(prevProps, prevState, snapshot) {
        console.log(
            'Component did update and received snapshot:',
            snapshot,
        )
    }
    render() {
        return (
            <span style={{ color: this.state.color }}>
                {this.state.time}
            </span>
        )
    }
```

```
        }
```

4. Then, define an `App` class component, which will be used for testing your
   previously created component. Add three buttons: one that will toggle the color
   property between red and blue and pass it as a prop to the `LifeCycleTime`
   component, another button for toggling the `dontUpdate` property in the state
   between true and false, which will then be passed as a prop to the
   `LifeCycleTime`, and finally, a button that when clicked will either mount or
   unmount the `LifeCycleTime` component:

```
class App extends React.Component {
    constructor(props) {
        super(props)
        this.state = {
            color: 'red',
            dontUpdate: false,
            unmount: false,
        }
        this.toggleColor = this.toggleColor.bind(this)
        this.toggleUpdate = this.toggleUpdate.bind(this)
        this.toggleUnmount = this.toggleUnmount.bind(this)
    }
    toggleColor() {
        this.setState((prevState) => ({
            color: prevState.color === 'red'
                ? 'blue'
                : 'red',
        }))
    }
    toggleUpdate() {
        this.setState((prevState) => ({
            dontUpdate: !prevState.dontUpdate,
        }))
    }
    toggleUnmount() {
        this.setState((prevState) => ({
            unmount: !prevState.unmount,
        }))
    }
    render() {
        const {
            color,
            dontUpdate,
            unmount,
        } = this.state
        return (
```

```
                    <React.Fragment>
                        {unmount === false && <LifeCycleTime
                            color={color}
                            dontUpdate={dontUpdate}
                        />}
                        <button onClick={this.toggleColor}>
                            Toggle color
                            {JSON.stringify({ color })}
                        </button>
                        <button onClick={this.toggleUpdate}>
                            Should update?
                            {JSON.stringify({ dontUpdate })}
                        </button>
                        <button onClick={this.toggleUnmount}>
                            Should unmount?
                            {JSON.stringify({ unmount })}
                        </button>
                    </React.Fragment>
                )
            }
        }
```

5. Render the application:

```
ReactDOM.render(
    <App />,
    document.querySelector('[role="main"]'),
)
```

6. Save the file.

Let's test it...

To see the previous work in action, perform the following steps::

1. Open a Terminal at the root of your project directory and run:

   npm start

2. Then, open a new tab in your web browser and go to:

   http://localhost:1337/

3. Use the buttons to toggle the state of the component and understand how the life cycle methods affect the component's functionality.

Working with React.PureComponent

`React.PureComponent` is similar to `React.Component`. The difference is that `React.Component` implements the `shouldComponentUpdate` life cycle method internally to make a shallow comparison of the `state` and `props` to decide if the component should update or not.

Getting ready

In this recipe, you will write two components, one extending `React.PureComponent`, and another extending `React.Component`, in order to see how they behave when the same properties are passed to them. Before you start, create a new `package.json` file with the following content:

```
{
  "scripts": {
    "start": "parcel serve -p 1337 index.html"
  },
  "devDependencies": {
    "babel-plugin-transform-class-properties": "6.24.1",
    "babel-preset-env": "1.6.1",
    "babel-preset-react": "6.24.1",
    "babel-core": "6.26.3",
    "parcel-bundler": "1.8.1",
    "react": "16.3.2",
    "react-dom": "16.3.2"
  }
}
```

Next, create a babel configuration file as `.babelrc`, adding the following content:

```
{
    "presets": ["env","react"],
    "plugins": ["transform-class-properties"]
}
```

Then, install the dependencies by opening a Terminal and running:

```
npm install
```

How to do it...

Build a React application to illustrate and understand better how React.PureComponent works. Create two components: one will extend React.Component while the other will extend React.PureComponent. Both components will be placed inside another React component named App that will update its state around every second. Using the life cycle method, componentDidUpdate, in both components, we will log on the console which one of them gets updated when the parent component App updates.

First, create an index.html file where the react application will be rendered:

1. Create a new file named index.html
2. Add the following HTML code:

```
<!DOCTYPE html>
<html lang="en">
<head>
    <meta charset="UTF-8">
    <title>React.PureComponent</title>
</head>
<body>
    <div role="main"></div>
    <script src="./pure-component.js"></script>
</body>
</html>
```

3. Save the file

Then, follow the next steps to build the React application:

1. Create a new file named pure-component.js.
2. Import the React and ReactDOM libraries:

```
import * as React from 'react'
import * as ReactDOM from 'react-dom'
```

3. Define a Button class component extending the React.PureComponent class:

```
class Button extends React.PureComponent {
    componentDidUpdate() {
        console.log('Button Component did update!')
    }
    render() {
        return (
            <button>{this.props.children}</button>
```

```
        )
    }
}
```

4. Define a `Text` class component extending the `React.Component` class:

```
class Text extends React.Component {
    componentDidUpdate() {
        console.log('Text Component did update!')
    }
    render() {
        return this.props.children
    }
}
```

5. Define a simple `App` component that will render both components. The `App` component will set a timer once it's mounted and update the state around every second:

```
class App extends React.Component {
    state = {
        counter: 0,
    }
    componentDidMount() {
        this.intervalId = setInterval(() => {
            this.setState(({ counter }) => ({
                counter: counter + 1,
            }))
        }, 1000)
    }
    componentWillUnmount() {
        clearInterval(this.intervalId)
    }
    render() {
        const { counter } = this.state
        return (
            <React.Fragment>
                <h1>Counter: {counter}</h1>
                <Text>I'm just a text</Text>
                <Button>I'm a button</Button>
            </React.Fragment>
        )
    }
}
```

6. Render the application:

```
ReactDOM.render(
    <App />,
    document.querySelector('[role="main"]'),
)
```

7. Save the file.

Let's test it...

To see the previous work in action, perform the following steps:

1. Open a Terminal at the root of your project directory and run:

   npm start

2. Then, open a new tab in your web browser and go to:

   `http://localhost:1337/`

3. The counter will increase by one around every second. Open the developer tools in your browser and check the console output. You should see the following:

   `[N] Text Component did update!`

How it works...

Because `React.PureComponent` implements the `shouldComponentUpdate`**life cycle method** internally, it doesn't update the `Button` component because its `state` or `props` have not changed. It does, however, update the `Text` component because `shouldComponentUpdate` returns `true` by default, telling React to update the component, even though its props or state have not changed.

React event handlers

React's event system uses internally a wrapper, called `SyntheticEvent`, around the native HTML DOM events for cross-browser support. React events follow the W3C spec, which can be found at `https://www.w3.org/TR/DOM-Level-3-Events/`.

React event names are camel-cased as opposed to HTML DOM events, which are lowercased. For instance, the HTML DOM event `onclick` would be called `onClick` in React. For a complete list of supported events, visit the React official documentation about events: `https://reactjs.org/docs/events.html`

Getting ready

In this recipe, you will write a component to see how it is defined and how it works. Before you start, create a new `package.json` file with the following content:

```
{
  "scripts": {
    "start": "parcel serve -p 1337 index.html"
  },
  "devDependencies": {
    "babel-plugin-transform-class-properties": "6.24.1",
    "babel-preset-env": "1.6.1",
    "babel-preset-react": "6.24.1",
    "babel-core": "6.26.3",
    "parcel-bundler": "1.8.1",
    "react": "16.3.2",
    "react-dom": "16.3.2"
  }
}
```

Next, create a babel configuration file as `.babelrc`, adding the following content:

```
{
    "presets": ["env","react"],
    "plugins": ["transform-class-properties"]
}
```

Then, install the dependencies by opening a Terminal and running:

```
npm install
```

How to do it...

Firstly, create an `index.html` file where the React application will be rendered:

1. Create a new file named `index.html`
2. Add the following HTML code:

```html
<!DOCTYPE html>
<html lang="en">
<head>
    <meta charset="UTF-8">
    <title>React Events Handlers</title>
</head>
<body>
    <div role="main"></div>
    <script src="./events.js"></script>
</body>
</html>
```

3. Save the file

Next, write a component defining an event handler for the `onClick` event:

1. Create a new file named `events.js`.
2. Import the React and ReactDOM libraries:

```js
import * as React from 'react'
import * as ReactDOM from 'react-dom'
```

3. Define a class component that will render a `h1` React element and a `button` React element, which will trigger the `onBtnClick` method whenever it's clicked:

```js
class App extends React.Component {
    constructor(props) {
        super(props)
        this.state = {
            title: 'Untitled',
        }
        this.onBtnClick = this.onBtnClick.bind(this)
    }
    onBtnClick() {
        this.setState({
            title: 'Hello there!',
        })
    }
    render() {
```

```
        return (
            <section>
                <h1>{this.state.title}</h1>
                <button onClick={this.onBtnClick}>
                    Click me to change the title
                </button>
            </section>
        )
    }
}
```

4. Render the application:

```
ReactDOM.render(
    <App />,
    document.querySelector('[role="main"]'),
)
```

5. Save the file.

Let's test it...

To see the application working, perform the following steps:

1. Open a Terminal at the root of your project directory and run:

   npm start

2. Then, open a new tab in your web browser and go to:

   `http://localhost:1337/`

3. Click on the button to change the title.

How it works...

React events are passed to React elements as `props`. For instance, we passed the `onClick` prop to the `button` React element and a reference to a callback function that we expect to be called when the user clicks on the button.

There's more...

Did you notice that we have been using the `bind` very often? When a method is passed as a prop to a child component, it loses the context of `this`, so binding to the context is necessary. Take the following example:

```
class Example {
    fn() { return this }
}
const examp = new Example()
const props = examp.fn
const bound = examp.fn.bind(examp)
console.log('1:', typeof examp.fn())
console.log('2:', typeof props())
console.log('3:', typeof bound())
```

The output displayed will be:

```
1: object
2: undefined
3: object
```

Even though the constant `props` has a reference to the `fn` method of the `examp` instance of the `Example` class, it loses the context of `this`. That's why binding allows you to keep the original context. In React, we bind a method to the original context of `this` to be able to use our own instance methods, such as `setState`, when passing the function down to child components. Otherwise, the context of `this` will be `undefined` and the function will fail.

Conditional rendering of components

Usually when building complex UIs, you would need to render a component or a React element according to the state or props received.

React components allow JavaScript to be executed within curly brackets and it can be used with the conditional ternary operator to decide which component or React element to render. For instance:

```
const Meal = ({ timeOfDay }) => (
    <span>{timeOfDay === 'noon'
        ? 'Pizza'
        : 'Sandwich'
    }</span>
)
```

This also could have been written as:

```
const Meal = ({ timeOfDay }) => (
    <span children={timeOfDay === 'noon'
        ? 'Pizza'
        : 'Sandwich'
    } />
)
```

If passing `"noon"` as the `timeOfDay` property value, it will generate the following HTML content:

```
<span>Pizza</span>
```

Or the following when the `timeOfDay` property is not set to `"noon"`:

```
<span>Sandwich</span>
```

Getting ready

In this recipe, you will build a component that that renders one of its children according to a given condition. Firstly, create a new `package.json` file with the following content:

```
{
  "scripts": {
    "start": "parcel serve -p 1337 index.html"
  },
  "devDependencies": {
    "babel-plugin-transform-class-properties": "6.24.1",
    "babel-preset-env": "1.6.1",
    "babel-preset-react": "6.24.1",
    "babel-core": "6.26.3",
    "parcel-bundler": "1.8.1",
    "react": "16.3.2",
    "react-dom": "16.3.2"
  }
}
```

Next, create a babel configuration file as `.babelrc`, adding the following content:

```
{
    "presets": ["env","react"],
    "plugins": ["transform-class-properties"]
}
```

Then, install the dependencies by opening a Terminal and running:

```
npm install
```

How to do it...

Write a React component that will decide which of two different React elements, given as `children` to your component, will be displayed according to a `condition` passed as a property. If the condition is true, then the first child is displayed. Otherwise, the second child should be displayed.

First, create an `index.html` file where the React application will be rendered:

1. Create a new file named `index.html`
2. Add the following HTML code:

```
<!DOCTYPE html>
<html lang="en">
<head>
    <meta charset="UTF-8">
    <title>Conditional Rendering</title>
</head>
<body>
    <div role="main"></div>
    <script src="./conditions.js"></script>
</body>
</html>
```

3. Save the file

Then, create a new file containing the logic of the React application and your component:

1. Create a new file named `conditions.js`
2. Import the React and ReactDOM libraries:

```
import * as React from 'react'
import * as ReactDOM from 'react-dom'
```

3. Define a functional component named `Toggle` that will receive a `condition` property that will be evaluated to define which React element to render. It expects to receive two React elements as children:

```
const Toggle = ({ condition, children }) => (
    condition
```

```
            ? children[0]
            : children[1]
    )
```

4. Define a class component named `App` that will render a React element based on
    the defined condition. When the button is clicked, it will toggle the `color` state:

```
class App extends React.Component {
    constructor(props) {
        super(props)
        this.state = {
            color: 'blue',
        }
        this.onClick = this.onClick.bind(this)
    }
    onClick() {
        this.setState(({ color }) => ({
            color: (color === 'blue') ? 'lime' : 'blue'
        }))
    }
    render() {
        const { color } = this.state
        return (
            <React.Fragment>
                <Toggle condition={color === 'blue'}>
                    <p style={{ color }}>Blue!</p>
                    <p style={{ color }}>Lime!</p>
                </Toggle>
                <button onClick={this.onClick}>
                    Toggle Colors
                </button>
            </React.Fragment>
        )
    }
}
```

5. Render the application:

```
ReactDOM.render(
    <App />,
    document.querySelector('[role="main"]'),
)
```

6. Save the file.

Let's test it...

To run and test the application, perform the following steps:

1. Open a Terminal at the root of your project directory and run:

   npm start

2. Then, open a new tab in your web browser and go to:

   `http://localhost:1337/`

3. Click on the button to toggle which React element is displayed

How it works...

Because the `children` property can be an array of React elements, we can access each individual React element and decide which one to render. We used the `condition` property to evaluate if the given condition is truthy to render the first React element. Otherwise, if the value is falsy, then the second React element is rendered.

Rendering lists with React

React allows you to pass a collection of React elements or components as `children` in the form of an array. For instance:

```
<ul>
    {[
        <li key={0}>One</li>,
        <li key={1}>Two</li>,
    ]}
</ul>
```

Collections of React elements or components must be given a special props property named `key`. This property lets React know which of the elements in the collection have changed, moved, or been removed in/from the array when an update occurs.

Getting ready

In this recipe, you will build a utility component that will map each item of an array to a component's props and render them as a list. Before you start, create a new `package.json` file with the following content:

```
{
  "scripts": {
    "start": "parcel serve -p 1337 index.html"
  },
  "devDependencies": {
    "babel-plugin-transform-class-properties": "6.24.1",
    "babel-preset-env": "1.6.1",
    "babel-preset-react": "6.24.1",
    "babel-core": "6.26.3",
    "parcel-bundler": "1.8.1",
    "react": "16.3.2",
    "react-dom": "16.3.2"
  }
}
```

Next, create a babel configuration file as `.babelrc`, adding the following content:

```
{
    "presets": ["env","react"],
    "plugins": ["transform-class-properties"]
}
```

Then, install the dependencies by opening a Terminal and running:

```
npm install
```

How to do it...

Create a React component named `MapArray`, which will do the job of mapping the items of an array to a React component.

First, create an `index.html` file where the React application will be rendered:

1. Create a new file named `index.html`
2. Add the following HTML code:

```
<!DOCTYPE html>
<html lang="en">
<head>
    <meta charset="UTF-8">
    <title>Rendering Lists</title>
</head>
<body>
    <div role="main"></div>
    <script src="./lists.js"></script>
</body>
</html>
```

3. Save the file

Then, perform the following steps to build the React application:

1. Create a new file named `lists.js`.
2. Import the React and ReactDOM libraries:

```
import * as React from 'react'
import * as ReactDOM from 'react-dom'
```

3. Define a functional component called `MapArray` that will expect to receive three properties: `from`, which is expected to be an array of values, `mapToProps`, which is expected to be a callback function for mapping values to properties, and lastly, `children`, which is expected to receive a React component where the values of the array will be mapped to:

```
const MapArray = ({
    from,
    mapToProps,
    children: Child,
}) => (
    <React.Fragment>
        {from.map((item) => (
            <Child {...mapToProps(item)} />
        ))}
    </React.Fragment>
)
```

4. Define a `TodoItem` component that expects to receive two properties, `done` and `label`:

```
const TodoItem = ({ done, label }) => (
    <li>
        <input type="checkbox" checked={done} readOnly />
        <label>{label}</label>
    </li>
)
```

5. Define an array that contains a to-do list of object values:

```
const list = [
    { id: 1, done: true, title: 'Study for Chinese exam' },
    { id: 2, done: false, title: 'Take a shower' },
    { id: 3, done: false, title: 'Finish chapter 6' },
]
```

6. Define a callback function that will map the array's object values to the expected properties of the `TodoItem` component. Rename the `id` property as `key`, and the `title` property as `label`:

```
const mapToProps = ({ id: key, done, title: label }) => ({
    key,
    done,
    label,
})
```

7. Define a `TodoListApp` component that will make use of the `MapArray` component to create an instance of `TodoItem` for every item in the to-do list array:

```
const TodoListApp = ({ items }) => (
    <ol>
        <MapArray from={list} mapToProps={mapToProps}>
            {TodoItem}
        </MapArray>
    </ol>
)
```

8. Render the application:

```
ReactDOM.render(
    <TodoListApp items={list} />,
    document.querySelector('[role="main"]'),
)
```

9. Save the file.

Let's test it...

To run and test the application, perform the following steps:

1. Open a Terminal at the root of your project directory and run:

   npm start

2. Then, open a new tab in your web browser and go to:

   `http://localhost:1337/`

3. A list of to-do items should be displayed:

List of to-do items

How it works...

Look at the following code:

```
<ol>
    <MapArray from={list} mapToProps={mapToProps}>
        {TodoItem}
    </MapArray>
</ol>
```

This works pretty much the same as writing:

```
<ol>
    <React.Fragment>
        {from.map((item) => (
            <TodoItem {...mapToProps(item) } />
        ))}
    </React.Fragment>
</ol>
```

However, `MapArray` acts as a helper component to do the same job while keeping the code more readable.

Have you noticed that the `TodoItem` component expects only two properties? However, we're also passing the `id` of the items as `key`. If the `key` property is not passed, then while rendering the components, a warning will be displayed.

Working with forms and inputs in React

Form-associated elements, such as `<input>` and `<textarea>`, usually maintain their own internal state and update it according to the user input. In React, when the input of a **form-associated element** is managed using the React state, it's called a **controlled component**.

By default, in React, if the `value` property of an input is not set, then the input internal state can be mutated by the user input. However, if the `value` property is set, then the input is read-only and it expects React to manage the user input by using the `onChange` React event and manage the input's state using the React state to update it if necessary. For example, this `input` React element will be rendered as read-only:

```
<input type="text" value="Ms.Huang Jx" />
```

However, because React expects to find an `onChange` event handler, the previous code will output a warning message on the console. To fix this, we can provide to the `onChange` property a callback function to handle the user input:

```
<input type="text" value="Ms.Huang Jx" onChange={event => null} />
```

Because the user input is handled by React and, in the previous example, we don't update the input's value, then the input will appear to be read-only. The previous code is similar to just setting a `readOnly` property instead of providing a useless `onChange` property.

React also allows you to define **uncontrolled components,** which basically keep out of React's control what or input how the input is updated. For instance, when a third-party library is used instead to act over the input, **uncontrolled components** have a property called `defaultValue,` which is similar to the `value` property. However, it lets the input control its internal state by the user input and not by React. That means a **form-associated element** with a `defaultValue` property allows its state to be mutated by the user input:

```
<input type="text" defaultValue="Ms.Huang Jx" />
```

As opposed to using the `value` property, you can now type in the input box to change its value because the internal state of the input is mutable.

Getting ready

In this recipe, you will build a simple login form component. Before you start, create a new `package.json` file with the following content:

```
{
  "scripts": {
    "start": "parcel serve -p 1337 index.html"
  },
  "devDependencies": {
    "babel-plugin-transform-class-properties": "6.24.1",
    "babel-preset-env": "1.6.1",
    "babel-preset-react": "6.24.1",
    "babel-core": "6.26.3",
    "parcel-bundler": "1.8.1",
    "react": "16.3.2",
    "react-dom": "16.3.2"
  }
}
```

Next, create a babel configuration file as `.babelrc`, adding the following content:

```
{
    "presets": ["env","react"],
    "plugins": ["transform-class-properties"]
}
```

Then, install the dependencies by opening a Terminal and running:

```
npm install
```

How to do it...

Define a class component named `LoginForm` that will handle `username` input and `password` input.

Firstly, create an `index.html` file where the React application will be rendered:

1. Create a new file named `index.html`
2. Add the following HTML code:

```
<!DOCTYPE html>
<html lang="en">
<head>
    <meta charset="UTF-8">
    <title>Forms and Inputs</title>
</head>
<body>
    <div role="main"></div>
    <script src="./forms.js"></script>
</body>
</html>
```

3. Save the file

Next, build the `LoginForm` component and use the power given to you by React *controlled components* over the input's state to also disallow numbers on the `username` input:

1. Create a new file named `forms.js`.
2. Import the React and ReactDOM libraries:

```
import * as React from 'react'
import * as ReactDOM from 'react-dom'
```

3. Define a class component named `LoginForm`. Within the class, define an event handler for the input change, and check the `username` input's value to disallow introducing numbers:

```
class LoginForm extends React.Component {
    constructor(props) {
        super(props)
        this.state = {
            username: '',
            password: '',
        }
        this.onChange = this.onChange.bind(this)
```

```
    }
    onChange(event) {
        const { name, value } = event.target
        this.setState({
            [name]: name === 'username'
                ? value.replace(/d/gi, '')
                : value
        })
    }
    render() {
        return (
            <form>
                <input
                    type="text"
                    name="username"
                    placeholder="Username"
                    value={this.state.username}
                    onChange={this.onChange}
                />
                <input
                    type="password"
                    name="password"
                    placeholder="Password"
                    value={this.state.password}
                    onChange={this.onChange}
                />
                <pre>
                    {JSON.stringify(this.state, null, 2)}
                </pre>
            </form>
        )
    }
}
```

4. Render the application:

```
ReactDOM.render(
    <LoginForm />,
    document.querySelector('[role="main"]'),
)
```

5. Save the file.

Let's test it...

To run and test the application, perform the following steps:

1. Open a Terminal at the root of your project directory and run:

   npm start

2. Then, open a new tab in your web browser and go to:

   `http://localhost:1337/`

3. Try to introduce a number in the `username` input to see how the validation against numbers is working

How it works...

We define an `onChange` event handler used in both input elements. However, we check if the input's name is `username` to decide if the validation should be applied. `RegExp` is used to test for numbers in the input and replace them with an empty string. That's why numbers are not displayed while typing on the `username` input.

Understanding refs and how to use them

In the usual workflow, React components communicate with their children by passing `props`. However, there are a few cases where it's needed to access the instance of a child to communicate or modify its behavior. React uses `refs` to allow us to access the instance of a child.

It's important to understand that React components' instances give you access to their instance methods and properties. However, an instance of a React element is an instance of an HTML DOM element. Refs are accessed by giving a `ref` attribute to the React component or React element. It expects the value to be a callback function that will be invoked once the instance is created, providing a reference to the instance in the first argument passed to the callback function.

React provides a helper function named `createRef` to define function callbacks for setting refs correctly. Take, for example, the following code, which obtains a reference of a React component and a React element:

```
class Span extends React.Component {
    render() {
        return <span>{this.props.children}</span>
    }
}
class App extends React.Component {
    rf1 = React.createRef()
    rf2 = React.createRef()
    componentDidMount() {
        const { rf1, rf2 } = this
        console.log(rf1.current instanceof HTMLSpanElement)
        console.log(rf2.current instanceof Span)
    }
    render() {
        return (
            <React.Fragment>
                <span ref={this.rf1} />
                <Span ref={this.rf2} />
            </React.Fragment>
        )
    }
}
```

In this example, the console will output `true` twice:

```
true // rf1.current instanceof HTMLSpanElement
true // rf2.current instanceof Span
```

This proves what we have just learned.

Functional components do not have `refs`. Thus, giving a `ref` property to a functional component will display a warning in the console and fail.

Refs are especially useful for working with *uncontrolled components* in the following cases:

- Integration with third-party libraries
- Accessing an HTML DOM element's native methods that are otherwise inaccessible from React, such as the `HTMLElement.focus()` method
- Using certain web APIs, such as the Selection Web API, the Web Animations API, and media playback methods

Getting ready

In this recipe, you will work with uncontrolled components and use refs to send a custom event to a form HTML element. Before you start, create a new `package.json` file with the following content:

```
{
  "scripts": {
    "start": "parcel serve -p 1337 index.html"
  },
  "devDependencies": {
    "babel-plugin-transform-class-properties": "6.24.1",
    "babel-preset-env": "1.6.1",
    "babel-preset-react": "6.24.1",
    "babel-core": "6.26.3",
    "parcel-bundler": "1.8.1",
    "react": "16.3.2",
    "react-dom": "16.3.2"
  }
}
```

Next, create a babel configuration file as `.babelrc`, adding the following content:

```
{
    "presets": ["env","react"],
    "plugins": ["transform-class-properties"]
}
```

Then, install the dependencies by opening a Terminal and running:

```
npm install
```

How to do it...

Define a `LoginForm` class component that will render a form with two inputs: one for a username and the other for a password. Include a button outside of the form React element, which will be used for triggering the `onSubmit` event on the form React element.

Firstly, create an `index.html` file where the React application will be rendered:

1. Create a new file named `index.html`
2. Add the following HTML code:

```
<!DOCTYPE html>
<html lang="en">
<head>
    <meta charset="UTF-8">
    <title>Refs</title>
</head>
<body>
    <div role="main"></div>
    <script src="./refs.js"></script>
</body>
</html>
```

3. Save the file

Now, start building the React application:

1. Create a new file named `refs.js`.
2. Import the React and ReactDOM libraries:

```
import * as React from 'react'
import * as ReactDOM from 'react-dom'
```

3. Define a class component named `LoginForm` that will render the form and a button that will trigger the `onSubmit` form event, using `refs`, when clicked:

```
class LoginForm extends React.Component {
    refForm = React.createRef()
    constructor(props) {
        super(props)
        this.state = {}
        this.onSubmit = this.onSubmit.bind(this)
        this.onClick = this.onClick.bind(this)
    }
    onSubmit(event) {
        const form = this.refForm.current
```

```
                const data = new FormData(form)
                this.setState({
                    user: data.get('user'),
                    pass: data.get('pass'),
                })
                event.preventDefault()
            }
            onClick(event) {
                const form = this.refForm.current
                form.dispatchEvent(new Event('submit'))
            }
            render() {
                const { onSubmit, onClick, refForm, state } = this
                return (
                    <React.Fragment>
                        <form onSubmit={onSubmit} ref={refForm}>
                            <input type="text" name="user" />
                            <input type="text" name="pass" />
                        </form>
                        <button onClick={onClick}>LogIn</button>
                        <pre>{JSON.stringify(state, null, 2)}</pre>
                    </React.Fragment>
                )
            }
        }
```

4. Render the application:

```
ReactDOM.render(
    <LoginForm />,
    document.querySelector('[role="main"]'),
)
```

5. Save the file.

Let's test it...

To run and test the application, perform the following steps:

1. Open a Terminal at the root of your project directory and run:

   npm start

2. Then, open a new tab in your web browser and go to:

   ```
   http://localhost:1337/
   ```

How it works...

1. Click on the `LogIn` button to test that the form `onSubmit` events gets triggered.
2. First, a reference to the instance of the form DOM element is kept in an instance property called `reform`.
3. Then, once the button is submitted, we use the `EventTarget` web API `dispatchEvent` method to dispatch a custom event `submit` on the form DOM element.
4. Then, the dispatched `submit` method is caught by the React `SyntheticEvent`.
5. Finally, React triggers the callback method passed to the form's `onSubmit` property.

Understanding React portals

React portals allow us to render child components in a different DOM element outside of the DOM tree generated by the parent component while keeping the React tree as if the component is inside the DOM tree generated by the parent component. For instance, even though child components are located in a different DOM node, the events generated in a child component bubble up to the React parent component.

React portals are created using the ReactDOM library's `createPortal` method and it has the same signature as the `render` method:

```
ReactDOM.createPortal(
    ReactComponent,
    DOMNode,
)
```

However, the difference between `render` and `createPortal` is that the latter returns a special tag that is used in the React tree to identify this element as a React portal and to use it as if it were a React element. For instance:

```
<article>
    {ReactDOM.createPortal(
        <h1>Example</h1>,
        document.querySelector('[id="heading"]'),
    )}
</article>
```

Getting ready

Before you start, create a new `package.json` file with the following content:

```
{
  "scripts": {
    "start": "parcel serve -p 1337 index.html"
  },
  "devDependencies": {
    "babel-plugin-transform-class-properties": "6.24.1",
    "babel-preset-env": "1.6.1",
    "babel-preset-react": "6.24.1",
    "babel-core": "6.26.3",
    "parcel-bundler": "1.8.1",
    "react": "16.3.2",
    "react-dom": "16.3.2"
  }
}
```

Next, create a babel configuration file as `.babelrc`, adding the following content:

```
{
    "presets": ["env","react"],
    "plugins": ["transform-class-properties"]
}
```

Then, install the dependencies by opening a Terminal and running:

```
npm install
```

How to do it...

First, create an `index.html` file where the React application will be rendered, containing as well an HTML `header` tag where a React portal element will be rendered:

1. Create a new file named `index.html`
2. Add the following HTML code:

```
<!DOCTYPE html>
<html lang="en">
<head>
    <meta charset="UTF-8">
    <title>Portals</title>
</head>
<body>
```

```
        <header id="heading"></header>
        <div role="main"></div>
        <script src="./portals.js"></script>
    </body>
    </html>
```

3. Save the file

Next, build a React application that will render a paragraph and an h1 HTML element outside of the tree to a `header` HTML element:

1. Create a new file named `portals.js`.
2. Import the React and ReactDOM libraries:

```
import * as React from 'react'
import * as ReactDOM from 'react-dom'
```

3. Define a functional component named `Header` and create a portal to render the `children` to a different DOM element:

```
const Header = () => ReactDOM.createPortal(
    <h1>React Portals</h1>,
    document.querySelector('[id="heading"]'),
)
```

4. Define a functional component named `App` that will render a React element and the `Header` React component:

```
const App = () => (
    <React.Fragment>
        <p>Hello World!</p>
        <Header />
    </React.Fragment>
)
```

5. Render the application:

```
ReactDOM.render(
    <App />,
    document.querySelector('[role="main"]'),
)
```

6. Save the file.

Let's test it...

To run and test the application, perform the following steps:

1. Open a Terminal at the root of your project directory and run:

   npm start

2. Then, open a new tab in your web browser and go to:

   ```
   http://localhost:1337/
   ```

3. The generated HTML DOM tree would look similar to this:

   ```
   <header id="heading">
      <h1>React Portals</h1>
   </header>
   <section role="main">
      <p>Hello World!</p>
   </section>
   ```

How it works...

Even though in the React tree the Header component appears to be rendered after the paragraph p HTML tag, the rendered Header component renders before it. That's because the Header component is actually rendered on a header HTML tag that appears before the section HTML tag where the main application is rendered.

Catching errors with error boundary components

Error boundary components are just React components that implement the componentDidCatch **life cycle method** to catch errors in their children. They catch errors in constructor methods when a class component is initialized but fails, in life cycle methods, and while rendering. Errors that cannot be caught are from asynchronous code, event handlers, and errors in the error component boundary itself.

The `componentDidCatch` life cycle method receives two arguments: the first one is an `error` object while the second received argument is an object containing a `componentStack` property with a friendly stack trace that describes where in the React tree a component failed.

Getting ready

In this recipe, you will build an error boundary component and provide a fallback UI when there is an error while rendering. Before you start, create a new `package.json` file with the following content:

```
{
  "scripts": {
    "start": "parcel serve -p 1337 index.html"
  },
  "devDependencies": {
    "babel-plugin-transform-class-properties": "6.24.1",
    "babel-preset-env": "1.6.1",
    "babel-preset-react": "6.24.1",
    "babel-core": "6.26.3",
    "parcel-bundler": "1.8.1",
    "react": "16.3.2",
    "react-dom": "16.3.2"
  }
}
```

Next, create a babel configuration file as `.babelrc`, adding the following content:

```
{
    "presets": ["env","react"],
    "plugins": ["transform-class-properties"]
}
```

Then, install the dependencies by opening a Terminal and running:

```
npm install
```

How to do it...

First, create an `index.html` file where the React application will be rendered:

1. Create a new file named `index.html`
2. Add the following HTML code:

```
<!DOCTYPE html>
<html lang="en">
<head>
    <meta charset="UTF-8">
    <title>Catching Errors</title>
</head>
<body>
    <div role="main"></div>
    <script src="./error-boundary.js"></script>
</body>
</html>
```

3. Save the file

Next, define an error boundary component that will catch errors and render a fallback UI displaying information where the error happened and the error message. Define as well an `App` component and create a `button` React element that when clicked will cause the application to fail while setting the state:

1. Create a new file named `error-boundary.js`.
2. Import the React and ReactDOM libraries:

```
import * as React from 'react'
import * as ReactDOM from 'react-dom'
```

3. Define an `ErrorBoundary` component that will display a fallback message when the application fails to render:

```
class ErrorBoundary extends React.Component {
    constructor(props) {
        super(props)
        this.state = {
            hasError: false,
            message: null,
            where: null,
        }
    }
    componentDidCatch(error, info) {
        this.setState({
```

```
            hasError: true,
            message: error.message,
            where: info.componentStack,
        })
    }
    render() {
        const { hasError, message, where } = this.state
        return (hasError
            ? <details style={{ whiteSpace: 'pre-wrap' }}>
                <summary>{message}</summary>
                <p>{where}</p>
            </details>
            : this.props.children
        )
    }
}
```

4. Define a class component named `App` that will render a `button` React element. Once the button is clicked, it will purposely throw an error:

```
class App extends React.Component {
    constructor(props) {
        super(props)
        this.onClick = this.onClick.bind(this)
    }
    onClick() {
        this.setState(() => {
            throw new Error('Error while setting state.')
        })
    }
    render() {
        return (
            <button onClick={this.onClick}>
                Buggy button!
            </button>
        )
    }
}
```

5. Render the application wrapping the `App` within the `ErrorBoundary` component:

```
ReactDOM.render(
    <ErrorBoundary>
        <App />
    </ErrorBoundary>,
    document.querySelector('[role="main"]'),
)
```

6. Save the file.

Let's test it...

To run and test the application, perform the following steps:

1. Open a Terminal at the root of your project directory and run:

   npm start

2. Then, open a new tab in your web browser and go to:

   `http://localhost:1337/`

3. Click on the `button` to cause the application to fail
4. A fallback UI is displayed showing the following error:

   Error while setting state.
   in App
   in ErrorBoundary

Type checking properties with PropTypes

React allows you to implement runtime type checking of components' properties. It's useful to catch bugs and make sure that your components are receiving `props` correctly. This can be easily done by just setting a static `propType` property on your components. For instance:

```
class MyComponent extends React.Component {
    static propTypes = {
        children: propTypes.string.isRequired,
    }
    render() {
        return<span>{this.props.children}</span>
```

```
        }
    }
```

The previous code will require `MyComponent`'s `children` property to be a `string`. Otherwise, if a different property type is given, React will display a warning in the console.

`propTypes`' methods are functions that get triggered when the component's instance is created to check if the given `props` match the `propTypes` schema.

`propTypes` have an extensive list of methods that can be used for the validation of properties. You can find the complete list in the React official documentation: `https:// reactjs.org/docs/typechecking-with-proptypes.html`.

Getting ready

In this recipe, you will see and write custom validation rules for checking property types. Before you start, create a new `package.json` file with the following content:

```
{
  "scripts": {
    "start": "parcel serve -p 1337 index.html"
  },
  "devDependencies": {
    "babel-core": "6.26.3",
    "babel-plugin-transform-class-properties": "6.24.1",
    "babel-preset-env": "1.6.1",
    "babel-preset-react": "6.24.1",
    "parcel-bundler": "1.8.1",
    "prop-types": "15.6.1",
    "react": "16.3.2",
    "react-dom": "16.3.2"
  }
}
```

Next, create a babel configuration file as `.babelrc`, adding the following content:

```
{
    "presets": ["env","react"],
    "plugins": ["transform-class-properties"]
}
```

Then, install the dependencies by opening a Terminal and running:

```
npm install
```

How to do it...

First, create an `index.html` file where the React application will be rendered:

1. Create a new file named `index.html`
2. Add the following HTML code:

```
<!DOCTYPE html>
<html lang="en">
<head>
    <meta charset="UTF-8">
    <title>Type Checking</title>
</head>
<body>
    <div role="main"></div>
    <script src="./type-checking.js"></script>
</body>
</html>
```

3. Save the file

Next, define a `Toggle` class component that expects to receive two React elements as `children`. Use `PropTypes` to create a custom validation rule to check that the `children` property is an array of React elements and the component is receiving exactly two React elements:

1. Create a new file named `type-checking.js`.
2. Import the React, ReactDOM, and `PropTypes` libraries:

```
import * as React from 'react'
import * as ReactDOM from 'react-dom'
import * as propTypes from 'prop-types'
```

3. Define a class component named `Toggle`. Use `propTypes` for type-checking the `condition` and `children` properties. Use a custom `propType` to check if `children` is an array of React elements and that it contains exactly two React elements:

```
class Toggle extends React.Component {
    static propTypes = {
        condition: propTypes.any.isRequired,
        children: (props, propName, componentName) => {
            const customPropTypes = {
                children: propTypes
                    .arrayOf(propTypes.element)
```

```
                    .isRequired
            }
            const isArrayOfElements = propTypes
                .checkPropTypes(
                    customPropTypes,
                    props,
                    propName,
                    componentName,
                )
            const children = props[propName]
            const count = React.Children.count(children)
            if (isArrayOfElements instanceof Error) {
                return isArrayOfElements
            } else if (count !== 2) {
                return new Error(
                    `"${componentName}"` +
                    ` expected ${propName}` +
                    ` to contain exactly 2 React elements`
                )
            }
        }
    }
    render() {
        const { condition, children } = this.props
        return condition ? children[0] : children[1]
    }
}
```

4. Define a class component named `App` that will render the `Toggle` component. Provide three React elements as its `children` and a `button` that when clicked will toggle the `value` property of state from `true` to `false` and vice versa:

```
class App extends React.Component {
    constructor(props) {
        super(props)
        this.state = { value: false }
        this.onClick = this.onClick.bind(this)
    }
    onClick() {
        this.setState(({ value }) => ({
            value: !value,
        }))
    }
    render() {
        const { value } = this.state
        return (
            <React.Fragment>
```

```
<Toggle condition={value}>
    <p style={{ color: 'blue' }}>Blue!</p>
    <p style={{ color: 'lime' }}>Lime!</p>
    <p style={{ color: 'pink' }}>Pink!</p>
</Toggle>
<button onClick={this.onClick}>
    Toggle Colors
</button>
        </React.Fragment>
    )
  }
}
```

5. Render the application:

```
ReactDOM.render(
    <App />,
    document.querySelector('[role="main"]'),
)
```

6. Save the file.

Let's test it...

To run and test the application, perform the following steps:

1. Open a Terminal at the root of your project directory and run:

   npm start

2. Then, open a new tab in your web browser and go to:

   http://localhost:1337/

3. The console in your browser will display the following warning:

   Warning: Failed prop type: "Toggle" expected children to contain exactly 2 React   elements
   **   in Toggle (created by App)**
   **   in App**

4. Clicking the `button` will toggle between the first two React elements while the third React element will be ignored

How it works...

We define a custom function validator for the `children` property. Inside the function, we first use the built-in `propTypes` functions to check if `children` is an array of React elements. If the result of the validation is not an instance of `Error`, then we use the React `Children`'s `count` utility method to know how many React elements were given and we return an error if the number of React elements in children is not 2.

There's more...

Did you notice that we used the `propTypes.checkPropTypes` method? It's a utility function that allows us to check for `propTypes` even outside React. For instance:

```
const pTypes = {
    name: propTypes.string.isRequired,
    age: propTypes.number.isRequired,
}
const props = {
    name: 'Huang Jx',
    age: 20,
}
propTypes.checkPropTypes(pTypes, props, 'property', 'props')
```

The `pTypes` object works as a schema providing validation functions from `propTypes`. The `props` constant is just a plain object containing properties defined in `pTypes`.

Running the previous example won't output any warning in the console since all properties in `props` are valid. However, change the `props` object to:

```
const props = {
    name: 20,
    age: 'Huang Jx',
}
```

Then we will see the following warning in the console output:

```
Warning: Failed property type: Invalid property `name` of type `number`
supplied to `props`, expected `string`.
Warning: Failed property type: Invalid property `age` of type `string`
supplied to `props`, expected `number`.
```

The `checkPropTypes` utility method has the following signature:

```
checkPropTypes(typeSpecs, values, location, componentName, getStack)
```

Here, `typeSpecs` refers to an object containing `propTypes` function validators. The `values` argument expects to receive an object whose values need to be validated against `typeSpecs`. `componentName` refers to the source's name, which usually is a component's name that is used in the warning message to display where the `Error` was originated. The last argument, `getStack,` is optional and it's expected to be a callback function that should return a `Stack Trace` that is added at the end of the warning message to better describe where exactly the error was originated.

`propTypes` are used only in development and for using the production build of React, you must set up the bundler to replace `process.env.NODE_ENV` with `"production"`. This way, `propTypes` are removed in the production build of your application.

Other Books You May Enjoy

If you enjoyed this book, you may be interested in these other books by Packt:

Full-Stack React Projects
Shama Hoque

ISBN: 978-1-78883-553-4

- Set up your development environment and develop a MERN application
- Implement user authentication and authorization using JSON Web Tokens
- Build a social media application by extending the basic MERN application
- Create an online marketplace application with shopping cart and Stripe payments
- Develop a media streaming application using MongoDB GridFS
- Implement server-side rendering with data to improve SEO
- Set up and use React 360 to develop user interfaces with VR capabilities
- Learn industry best practices to make MERN stack applications reliable and scalable

React 16 Essentials - Second Edition
Artemij Fedosejev, Adam Boduch

ISBN: 978-1-78712-604-6

- Learn to code React 16 with hands-on examples and clear tutorials
- Install powerful React 16 tools to make development much more efficient
- Understand the impact of React Fiber today and the future of your web development
- Utilize the Redux application architecture with your React components
- Create React 16 elements with properties and children
- Get started with stateless and stateful React components
- Use JSX to speed up your React 16 development process
- Add reactivity to your React 16 components with lifecycle methods
- Test your React 16 components with the Jest test framework

Leave a review - let other readers know what you think

Please share your thoughts on this book with others by leaving a review on the site that you bought it from. If you purchased the book from Amazon, please leave us an honest review on this book's Amazon page. This is vital so that other potential readers can see and use your unbiased opinion to make purchasing decisions, we can understand what our customers think about our products, and our authors can see your feedback on the title that they have worked with Packt to create. It will only take a few minutes of your time, but is valuable to other potential customers, our authors, and Packt. Thank you!

Index

P

path-to-regexp
  reference 22
principles, Redux
  pure functions, used for making changes 162
  read-only state 162
  single source of truth 162
PropTypes
  type checking properties, using with 272, 276, 278

Q

query builders, Mongoose
  using 78, 80

R

React components
  class components 221
  expressions 222
  functional components 221
React elements 220
React event handlers 243, 246
React portals 265, 267, 268
React.PureComponent
  working with 240, 243
React
  about 220
  forms, working with 256, 260
  input, working with 256, 260
  used, for rendering lists 251, 255, 256
reducer functions
  defining 165, 168, 171
  working 172
reducers
  combining 184
  splitting 184
Redux DevTools 205
Redux DevTools Extension
  reference 199
Redux middleware
  about 205
  testing 209
  using 207
  working 209

Redux store enhancers
  about 195
  working 199
  writing 195
Redux store
  creating 172, 173, 177
  testing 177, 178
Redux Thunk
  reference 217
Redux
  used, for time traveling 199, 202, 203
refs
  about 260
  using 260
REPL (Read-Eval-Print Loop) 102
Representation State Transfer (REST) 68
request methods
  features 17
RESTful API
  building, for managing users with ExpressJS 102
  building, for managing users with Mongoose 102
route handlers 20
route methods 18
route methods, ExpressJS
  used, for performing CRUD operations 68, 70, 73
router-level middleware functions
  working 34
  writing 31, 33
router
  about 23
  used, for creating modular application 23, 25

S

schemas, Mongoose
  custom validator, writing 97, 99, 101
Separation of Concern (SoC) 9
serve-static module
  reference 37
socket object 122
Socket.IO events
  about 121
  client events 123, 125, 127
  server events 122
  working 127

Made in the USA
Middletown, DE
08 September 2018